C000242837

# ROYAL COURT

**Royal Court Theatre presents**

# TERRORISM

by **the Presnyakov Brothers**
Translated by Sasha Dugdale

First performance at the Royal Court Jerwood Theatre Upstairs
Sloane Square, London on 10 March 2003.

Terrorism is produced as a Genesis Project with additional support from the British Council.

# TERRORISM

by **the Presnyakov Brothers**
Translated by Sasha Dugdale

Cast in order of appearance

Scene 1
Man in Military Uniform **Gary Oliver**, Passenger **Ian Dunn**,
Passenger 1 **Alan Williams**, Passenger 2 **Paul Hilton**

Scene 2
Woman **Suzan Sylvester**, Man **Paul Hilton**

Scene 3
Man **Paul Ready**, Woman **Sheila Reid**, Woman 2 **Di Botcher**,
Woman 3 **Suzan Sylvester**, Woman 4 **Sarah Cattle**,
Male Staff Member **Gary Oliver**, Psychologist **Alan Williams**

Scene 4
Woman 1 **Sheila Reid**, Woman 2 **Di Botcher**, Man **Ian Dunn**

Scene 5
Man 1 **Paul Hilton**, Man 2 **Ian Dunn**, Man 3 **Gary Oliver**,
Man 4 **Paul Ready**, Man 5 **Alan Williams**

Scene 6
Passenger **Ian Dunn**, Passenger1 **Alan Williams**,
Passenger 2 **Paul Hilton**, Air Hostess **Di Botcher**


Director **Ramin Gray**
Designer **Hildegard Bechtler**
Lighting Designer **Johanna Town**
Sound Designers **Emma Laxton, Ian Dickinson**
Assistant Director **Bijan Sheibani**
Assistant Designer **Luke Smith**
Casting **Lisa Makin, Amy Ball**
Production Manager **Sue Bird**
Stage Managers **Nicole Keighley, Louise McDermott**
Costume Supervisor **Jemimah Tomlinson**
Fight Director **Terry King**
Company Voice Work **Patsy Rodenburg**

The Royal Court Theatre would like to thank the following for their help with this production:
Vaughan Melzer at the Russian Mirror.
Wardrobe care by Persil and Comfort courtesy of Lever Fabergé.

## THE COMPANY

**Presynakov Brothers** (writers)
The Presynakov Brothers were born in Sverdlovsk, Siberia. They created the Gorky Urals State University's Youth Theatre, where they produce new and experimental theatre. Terrorism was produced at the Moscow Arts Theatre in November 2002. They are connected with the New Writing project in Russia inspired by the Royal Court and the British Council. We Shall Overcome, a short political play commissioned by the Royal Court, was seen as part of the International Playwrights Season 2002.

**Hildegard Bechtler** (designer)
For the Royal Court: Blasted, The Changing Room.
Other theatre includes: The Merchant of Venice, King Lear (RNT); La Maison de la Puppée (Theatre de l'Europe, Paris); Footfalls (Garrick); The St.Pancras Project (Lift); Richard II (RNT/Bobigny, Paris); Electra (RSC/Riverside/Bobigny, Paris); Hedda Gabler (Abbey, Dublin/Playhouse, London); Coriolanus (Salzburg Festival).
Film and television includes: The Merchant of Venice, Richard II, The Wasteland, Hedda Gabler, Coming Up Roses, Business As Usual.
Opera includes: The Ring Cycle: Das Rheingold, Walküre, Siegfried and Gotterdammerung (Spring· 2003), (Scottish Opera/Edinburgh Festival); Lady Macbeth of Mtsensk (Sidney Opera House); Paul Bunyan (ROH); War & Peace, Boris Gudonov, Peter Grimes, Lohengrin, The Bacchae (ENO); Dialogues Des Carmelites (Japan/Paris Opera); Simon Boccanegra, Peter Grimes (Staatsoper, Munich); Don Carlos, Wozzeck, Katya Kabanova (Opera North); Don Giovanni (Glyndebourne); La Wally (Bregenz Festival/ Amsterdam Musik Theatre).

**Di Botcher**
For the Royal Court: Black Milk.
Theatre includes: Beauty and the Beast (Dominion); Cats (New London); Cardiff East, Sunday in the Park with George, A Little Night Music, Under Milk Wood, The Absence of War, Sweeney Todd (RNT); Kes, The Frogs (RNT Studio); A Midsummer Night's Dream, Speculators, Lady Audley's Secret, Richard III (RSC); Card Boys (Bush); Flesh and Blood (Hampstead); The Oyster Catchers (Swansea); Into the Woods (Manchester); Moll Flanders (Colchester); Small Change (Haymarket, Basingstoke).
Television includes: Cruise of the Gods, Belonging (series three and four), 'Orrible, People Like Us, Fun at the Funeral Parlour, Light in the City, Alistair McGowan's Big Impression, Sunburn, Rhinoceros, Kavanagh QC, The Silent Twins, The Bill, District Nurse, Harpur and Iles, The Armando Ianucci Show, Casualty, Tipping the Velvet, High Hopes.
Film includes: Twin Town, All or Nothing, Life and Debt.
Radio includes: An Easy Game to Play, Lord of Misrule, A Bizarre Sort of Child, Night People, Imperial Palace.

**Sarah Cattle**
For the Royal Court: Black Milk, Made of Stone, Naturalised.
Other theatre includes: Inside Out (Clean Break); Boeing, Boeing (Lyceum, Crewe); Peril at End House (Grand, Wolverhampton); American Days (Mill Studio, Guildford); A Midsummer Night's Dream (Chilworth Manor).
Television includes: Rockface, Linda Green.
Film includes: Silent Cry, Hans Christian Anderson.

**Ian Dickinson** (sound designer)
For the Royal Court: Black Milk, Crazyblackmuthafuckin'self, Caryl Churchill Season, Imprint, Mother Teresa is Dead, Push Up, Workers Writes, Fucking Games, Herons, Cutting Through the Carnival.
Other theatre includes: Port (Royal Exchange Manchester); Night of the Soul (RSC Barbican); Eyes of the Kappa (Gate); Crime and Punishment in Dalston (Arcola Theatre); Search and Destroy (New End, Hampstead); Phaedra, Three Sisters, The Shaughraun, Writer's Cramp (Royal Lyceum, Edinburgh); The Whore's Dream (RSC Fringe, Edinburgh); As You Like It, An Experienced Woman Gives Advice, Present Laughter, The Philadelphia Story, Wolks World, Poor Superman, Martin Yesterday, Fast Food, Coyote Ugly, Prizenight (Royal Exchange, Manchester).
Ian is Head of Sound at the Royal Court.

**Sasha Dugdale** (translator)
Sasha has translated several Russian plays for the Royal Court, including How I Ate a Dog by Evgeny Grishkovets, Vassily Sigarev's Black Milk and Plasticine.

**Ian Dunn**
For the Royal Court: Fucking Games, Toast, I Am Yours, Babies, Six Degrees of Separation (& Comedy).
Other theatre includes: Luminosity, Love Play (RSC Pit); Chips with Everything, Somewhere (RNT); Our Boys (Donmar/Derby Playhouse); Hidden Laughter (Vaudeville); Forget Me Not Lane (Greenwich); Invisible Friends, Wolf At the Door, Brighton Beach Memoirs (Scarborough).
Television includes: Girls in Love, Trust, London's Burning, Peak Practice, Bad Girls, Holby City, The Bill, Reach for the Moon, Bliss, Stone, Scissors & Paper, Gulliver's Travels, Shine on Harvey Moon, Casualty, Desmonds, Jackanory: Gulf, The Merrihill

Millionaires, A Touch of Frost, Soldier Soldier, Children of the North, Sweet: Capital Lives. Film includes: American Friends, Bye Bye Baby.

**Ramin Gray** (director)
International Associate of the Royal Court. For the Royal Court: Night Owls, Just A Bloke (Imprint, Young Writers Festival 2002), Push Up (International Playwrights 2002), How I Ate a Dog (International Playwrights 2000), Daughters (Choice, Young Writers Festival 1998). Other theatre includes: The Child, The Invisible Woman (Gate); Cat and Mouse (Sheep) (Théâtre National de l'Odéon, Paris and Gate, London); Autumn and Winter (Man in the Moon); A Message for the Broken-Hearted (Liverpool Playhouse & BAC); At Fifty She Discovered the Sea, Harry's Bag, Pig's Ear, A View from the Bridge (Liverpool Playhouse); , The Malcontent (Latchmere Theatre).

**Paul Hilton**
For the Royal Court: Mountain Language. Other theatre includes: The Daughter-in-Law (Young Vic); The Homecoming, Les Blancs, Ghosts (Royal Exchange); Oresteia (RNT); The Storm (Almeida); The Three Sisters (Oxford Stage Co. & Whitehall); As You Like It, A Mad World My Masters (Globe and Tokyo); The Mysteries, Romeo and Juliet, The Cherry Orchard, Richard I I I, Woyzeck, Endgame (RSC); Twelfth Night, A Small Family Business, Stone Free (Bristol Old Vic).
Film and television includes: Purgation, The Bill. Radio includes: The Old Curiosity Shop, Antony & Cleopatra, As You Like It, The White Guard, Robin Hood's Revenge.

**Emma Laxton** (sound designer)
As sound operator, for the Royal Court: Boy Gets Girl, Dublin Carol, The Country, The Glory of Living, Toast, I Just Stopped By To See The Man.
As sound designer, other theatre includes: As You Like It, Romeo and Juliet (Regent's Park Open Air Theatre).
As sound operator, other theatre includes: Henry VI Part 1, 2 & 3, Richard I I I (Young Vic); Tartuffe, No Man's Land, The Wonder of Sex (RNT); A Midsummer Night's Dream, Love's Labour's Lost, Where's Charley ?, The Pirates of Penzance, Oh What A Lovely War (Regent's Park Open Air Theatre); Mnemonic (Complicite /Riverside Studios), Light (Complicite /Almeida, UK tour, Stockholm and Dublin theatre festivals).

**Gary Oliver**
For the Royal Court: Black Milk.
Theatre includes: A Streetcar Named Desire,

Sing Yer Heart Out for the Lads, The Cherry Orchard (RNT); Angels in America (Library Theatre); Squash, Then What (Old Red Lion); Comedy of Errors (RSC tour/Young Vic); Unidentified Human Remains (Royal Exchange); Salvation (Gate); The Fire Raisers, The Slow Approach of Night (Arts Threshold); The Lizzie Play (Theatre Clwyd & tour); Look Back in Anger, King Lear, Endgame (Wink Productions); Romeo & Juliet (Factotum Touring Company); Shoemaker's Wonderful Wife (BAC/Ragazzi Theatre Company); Puppet Play of Don Christabel (Ragazzi Theatre Company); The Importance of Being Earnest (Stephen Joseph Theatre).
Television includes: The Bill, Kavanagh QC, Casualty, Heartbeat, Soldier Soldier, Eastenders, Rules of Engagement, Discoveries of the World. Film includes: Horizontal Man.

**Paul Ready**
For the Royal Court: Black Milk, Crazyblackmuthafuckin'self.
Theatre includes: Romeo & Juliet (Liverpool Playhouse); Mother Clapp's Molly House (RNT/Aldwych); Twelfth Night (Liverpool Playhouse/Everyman); Cuckoos (Gate/RNT Studio); The Beggar's Opera (Broomhill Opera/ Wilton's Music Hall).
Television includes: Jeffrey Archer: The Truth, Heartbeat, Tipping the Velvet, Chambers, Harry Enfield Presents, Princess of Thieves, Poirot, Plain Jane, The Practice.
Film includes: Maybe Baby, Angels & Insects.

**Sheila Reid**
For the Royal Court: Black Milk, The Gentle Avalanche, Small Change, My Mother Said I Never Should.
Theatre includes: The Good Hope, Sweeney Todd, Caritas, Three Sisters, Hedda Gabler, The Crucible, Love's Labour's Lost, Othello, The Beaux Stratagem (RNT); Tartuffe, The Wood Demon, Lear, Ruling The Roost (The Actors Company); Cousin Vladimir, Romeo & Juliet, 'Tis Pity She's a Whore, King Baby (RSC); When I Was a Girl I Used to Scream and Shout (Whitehall/Bush); The Marshalling Yard, One Flea Spare (Bush); Façades, Crime and Punishment (Lyric); The Winter Guest (West Yorkshire Playhouse/Almeida); Martin Guerre (Prince Charles); Steaming (Piccadilly); Misalliance (Chichester); The Importance of Being Earnest (Chichester/Haymarket); Snake in the Grass (Peter Hall Company/Old Vic); Separate Tables, Up in the Eighties (King's Head); Into the Woods (Donmar); The Circle (Oxford Stage Company); Abandonment (Traverse); The Actress and the Bishop, If I'm Glad You'll Be Frank (Young Vic). Television includes: Flickers, Get Lost,

The Emigrants, Taggart, Dr Finlay, Oliver's Travels, The Cruel Train, Ghostbusters of East Finchley, My Wonderful Life, Where the Heart Is, The Sleeper, Monarch of the Glen, Midsomer Murders, The Bill.
Film includes: The Touch, Brazil, American Friends, Sir Henry at Rawlinson's End, Othello, Five Days One Summer, The Winter Guest, Watch That Man, Still Crazy, Felicia's Journey, Mrs Caldicot's Cabbage War.
Radio includes: The House, Colville & Soames, Villette.

**Bijan Sheibani** (assistant director)
As director, theatre includes: The Lover (BT, Oxford); Peace for our Time (Cockpit); Summer (Lion and Unicorn); The Stoning (BAC); Have I None (Southwark Playhouse).

**Suzan Sylvester**
For the Royal Court: Black Milk, Cleansed.
Other theatre includes: The Real Thing (tour); The Secret Rapture (Minerva, Chichester); Betrayal (Northcott, Exeter); Shang-a-Lang (tour); Card Boys (Bush); Terms of Abuse (Hampstead); The Reckless are Dying Out (Lyric); The House of Bernada Alba (Theatr Clwyd); Yiddish Trojan Women, Kindertransport (Cockpit); Three Sisters (Chichester); Love's Labour's Lost (Royal Exchange); Life is a Dream (West Yorkshire Playhouse); All My Sons, Romeo and Juliet (Young Vic); The Glass Menagerie (Young Vic/tour); An Enemy of the People (Young Vic/Playhouse); As You Like It, The Seagull, The Government Inspector (Crucible); Pericles, All's Well That Ends Well (RSC); 'Tis Pity She's a Whore, A Small Family Business, Tons of Money (RNT); A View from the Bridge (RNT/Aldwych).
Television includes: The Bill, Doctors, Casualty, Where the Heart Is, Maisie Raine, Touch of Frost, London's Burning, Holding On, Wycliffe, Pie in the Sky, Casualty, Peak Practice, Rides, Mysterioso, Call Me Mister.
Film includes: Streets of Yesterday.
Radio includes: Pentecost, Macbeth, The Last Dare, The Rover.
Awards include: Laurence Olivier Award for Most Promising Newcomer for A View from the Bridge.

**Johanna Town** (lighting designer)
Johanna has been Head of Lighting for the Royal Court since 1990 and has designed extensively for the company. Productions include: Caryl Churchill's Shorts, Where Do We Live, Plasticine, Fucking Games, Nightingale and Chase, I Just Stopped By To See the Man, Under the Blue Sky, Mr Kolpert, Other People, Blue Heart (& Out of Joint), Pale Horse, The Kitchen, Faith Healer.
Other recent theatre designs include: She Stoops to Conquer/A Laughing Matter, Hinterland(Out of Joint/RNT); Top Girls (Aldwych/OSC tour); Popcorn, Les Liaison Dangereuses, Playboy of the Western World (Liverpool Playhouse); Feelgood (Out of Joint/Hampstead/Garrick); Rita, Sue and Bob Too, A State Affair (Out of Joint/Soho Theatre); Arabian Nights (New Victory, New York); Ghosts (Royal Exchange Theatre); Our Lady of Sligo (Irish Repertory Theatre, New York); Rose (RNT/Broadway); Little Malcolm (Hampstead/West End).

**Alan Williams**
For the Royal Court: Black Milk; Crave (Paines Plough and Bright Ltd tour), Local, Bed of Roses, Weekend After Next (Hull Truck tour).
Other theatre includes: The Inland Sea (Oxford Stage Company); The Sea (Chichester Festival); The Jew of Malta (Almeida & tour); The Rib Cage, To the Chicago Abyss (Manchester Royal Exchange); Kiss the Sky (Bush); Vigil (Arts Club Theatre, Vancouver); The Darling Family (Theatre Passe Muraille, Toronto); White Dogs of Texas (Taragon Theatre, Toronto & tour); The Cockroach Trilogy (Hull Truck tour UK/ US/Canada); Having a Ball (Liverpool Playhouse); Mean Streaks (Hull Truck tour/Bush); Small Ads (King's Head); Mary Barnes (Birmingham Rep); Prejudice, Eejits (Liverpool Everyman); Bridget's House (Hull Truck tour).
Television includes: Peterloo, Serious and Organised, Paradise Heights, Wire in the Blood, Sirens, The Bill, Peak Practice, Coronation Street, The Mayor of Casterbridge, Love in a Cold Climate, Badger, Always & Everyone, Touching Evil, Getting Hurt, The Scold's Bridle, Wycliffe.
Film includes: Bright Young Things, Heartlands, All Or Nothing, Elephant Juice, Among Giants, The Cockroach that Ate Cincinnati, Coleslaw, The Darling Family, Daughters of the Country.
Radio includes: Five Letters Home to Elizabeth.

## THE ENGLISH STAGE COMPANY AT THE ROYAL COURT

The English Stage Company at the Royal Court opened in 1956 as a subsidised theatre producing new British plays, international plays and some classical revivals.

The first artistic director George Devine aimed to create a writers' theatre, 'a place where the dramatist is acknowledged as the fundamental creative force in the theatre and where the play is more important than the actors, the director, the designer'. The urgent need was to find a contemporary style in which the play, the acting, direction and design are all combined. He believed that 'the battle will be a long one to continue to create the right conditions for writers to work in'.

Devine aimed to discover 'hard-hitting, uncompromising writers whose plays are stimulating, provocative and exciting'. The Royal Court production of John Osborne's Look Back in Anger in May 1956 is now seen as the decisive starting point of modern British drama and the policy created a new generation of British playwrights. The first wave included John Osborne, Arnold Wesker, John Arden, Ann Jellicoe, N F Simpson and Edward Bond. Early seasons included new international plays by Bertolt Brecht, Eugène Ionesco, Samuel Beckett, Jean-Paul Sartre and Marguerite Duras.

The theatre started with the 400-seat proscenium arch Theatre Downstairs, and then in 1969 opened a second theatre, the studio Theatre Upstairs. It frequently transfers productions to the West End, such as Caryl Churchill's Far Away, Conor McPherson's The Weir, Kevin Elyot's Mouth to Mouth and My Night With Reg and also co-produces plays, such as Sebastian Barry's The Steward of Christendom and Mark Ravenhill's Shopping and Fucking (with Out of Joint), Martin McDonagh's The Beauty Queen Of Leenane (with Druid Theatre Company), Ayub Khan-Din's East is East (with Tamasha Theatre Company, and now a feature film).

Since 1994 the Royal Court's artistic policy has again been vigorously directed to finding and producing a new generation of playwrights. The writers include Joe Penhall, Rebecca Prichard, Michael Wynne, Nick Grosso, Judy Upton, Meredith Oakes, Sarah Kane, Anthony Neilson, Judith Johnson, James Stock, Jez Butterworth, Marina Carr, Phyllis Nagy, Simon Block, Martin McDonagh, Mark Ravenhill, Ayub Khan-Din, Tamantha Hammerschlag, Jess Walters, Che Walker, Conor McPherson, Simon Stephens, Richard Bean, Roy Williams, Gary Mitchell, Mick Mahoney, Rebecca Gilman, Christopher Shinn,

Kia Corthron, David Gieselmann, Marius von Mayenburg, David Eldridge, Leo Butler, Zinnie Harris, Grae Cleugh, Roland Schimmelpfennig, Vassily Sigarev and DeObia Oparei. This expanded programme of new plays has been made possible through the support of A.S.K Theater Projects, the Jerwood Charitable Foundation, the Genesis Foundation, the American Friends of the Royal Court Theatre and many in association with the Royal National Theatre Studio and the British Council.

In recent years there have been record-breaking productions at the box office, with capacity houses for Caryl Churchill's A Number, Jez Butterworth's The Night Heron, Rebecca Gilman's Boy Gets Girl, Kevin Elyot's Mouth To Mouth, David Hare's My Zinc Bed and Conor McPherson's The Weir, which transferred to the West End in October 1998 and ran for nearly two years at the Duke of York's Theatre.

The newly refurbished theatre in Sloane Square opened in February 2000, with a policy still inspired by George Devine.

## INTERNATIONAL PLAYWRIGHTS

Since 1992 the Royal Court has placed a renewed emphasis on the development of international work and a creative dialogue now exists with Cuba, Brazil, France, Germany, India, Palestine, Russia, Spain, Uganda and the United States. Many of these projects are supported by the British Council and the Genesis Foundation.

The Royal Court's exchange with Russian new writing began in 1999 and since then the Royal Court has led a number of workshops in Moscow, Novosibirsk and Ykaterinburg. Extracts from one of the projects developed in Russia, Moscow Open City, were performed as part of the International Playwrights Season 2000. In May 2001 the Royal Court presented a week of rehearsed readings, New Plays from Russia. In March 2002 Plasticine by Vassily Sigarev was produced as part of the International Playwrights Season. The Presnyakov Brothers were commissioned to write a short play, We Shall Overcome, as part of the Human Rights Focus of the 2002 International Playwrights Season.

International Playwrights: FOCUS RUSSIA is produced by the Royal Court International Department:
Associate Director **Elyse Dodgson**
International Administrator **Ushi Bagga**
International Associate **Ramin Gray**

# AWARDS FOR
# THE ROYAL COURT

Jez Butterworth won the 1995 George Devine Award, the Writers' Guild New Writer of the Year Award, the Evening Standard Award for Most Promising Playwright and the Olivier Award for Best Comedy for Mojo. The Royal Court was the overall winner of the 1995 Prudential Award for the Arts for creativity, excellence, innovation and accessibility. The Royal Court Theatre Upstairs won the 1995 Peter Brook Empty Space Award for innovation and excellence in theatre.

Michael Wynne won the 1996 Meyer-Whitworth Award for The Knocky. Martin McDonagh won the 1996 George Devine Award, the 1996 Writers' Guild Best Fringe Play Award, the 1996 Critics' Circle Award and the 1996 Evening Standard Award for Most Promising Playwright for The Beauty Queen of Leenane. Marina Carr won the 19th Susan Smith Blackburn Prize (1996/7) for Portia Coughlan. Conor McPherson won the 1997 George Devine Award, the 1997 Critics' Circle Award and the 1997 Evening Standard Award for Most Promising Playwright for The Weir. Ayub Khan-Din won the 1997 Writers' Guild Awards for Best West End Play and Writers' Guild New Writer of the Year and the 1996 John Whiting Award for East is East (co-production with Tamasha).

At the 1998 Tony Awards, Martin McDonagh's The Beauty Queen of Leenane (co-production with Druid Theatre Company) won four awards including Garry Hynes for Best Director and was nominated for a further two. Eugene Ionesco's The Chairs (co-production with Theatre de Complicite) was nominated for six Tony awards. David Hare won the 1998 Time Out Live Award for Outstanding Achievement and six awards in New York including the Drama League, Drama Desk and New York Critics Circle Award for Via Dolorosa. Sarah Kane won the 1998 Arts Foundation Fellowship in Playwriting. Rebecca Prichard won the 1998 Critics' Circle Award for Most Promising Playwright for Yard Gal (co-production with Clean Break).
Conor McPherson won the 1999 Olivier Award for Best New Play for The Weir. The Royal Court won the 1999 ITI Award for Excellence in International Theatre. Sarah Kane's Cleansed was judged Best Foreign Language Play in 1999 by Theater Heute in Germany. Gary Mitchell won the 1999 Pearson Best Play Award for Trust. Rebecca Gilman was joint winner of the 1999 George Devine Award and won the 1999 Evening Standard Award for Most Promising Playwright for The Glory of Living.

In 1999, the Royal Court won the European theatre prize New Theatrical Realities, presented at Taormina Arte in Sicily, for its efforts in recent years in discovering and producing the work of young British dramatists.

Roy Williams and Gary Mitchell won the George Devine Award 2000 for Most Promising Playwright for Lift Off and The Force of Change respectively. At the Barclays Theatre Awards 2000 presented by the TMA, Richard Wilson won the Best Director Award for David Gieselmann's Mr Kolpert and Jeremy Herbert won the Best Designer Award for Sarah Kane's 4.48 Psychosis. Gary Mitchell won the Evening Standard's Charles Wintour Award 2000 for Most Promising Playwright for The Force of Change. Stephen Jeffreys' I Just Stopped by to See The Man won an AT&T: On Stage Award 2000.

David Eldridge's Under the Blue Sky won the Time Out Live Award 2001 for Best New Play in the West End. Leo Butler won the George Devine Award 2001 for Most Promising Playwright for Redundant. Roy Williams won the Evening Standard's Charles Wintour Award 2001 for Most Promising Playwright for Clubland. Grae Cleugh won the 2001 Olivier Award for Most Promising Playwright for Fucking Games. Richard Bean was joint winner of the George Devine Award 2002 for Most Promising Playwright for Under the Whaleback. Caryl Churchill won the 2002 Evening Standard Award for Best New Play for A Number. Vassily Sigarev won the 2002 Evening Standard Charles Wintour Award for Most Promising Playwright for Plasticine. Ian MacNeil won the 2002 Evening Standard Award for Best Design for A Number and Plasticine. Peter Gill won the 2002 Critics' Circle Award for Best New Play for The York Realist (English Touring Theatre).

# ROYAL COURT BOOKSHOP

The bookshop offers a wide range of playtexts and theatre books, with over 1,000 titles. Located in the downstairs Bar and Food area, the bookshop is open Monday to Saturday, afternoons and evenings.

Many Royal Court playtexts are available for just £2 including works by Harold Pinter, Caryl Churchill, Rebecca Gilman, Martin Crimp, Sarah Kane, Conor McPherson, Ayub Khan-Din, Timberlake Wertenbaker and Roy Williams.

For information on titles and special events, Email: bookshop@royalcourttheatre.com
Tel: 020 7565 5024

## REBUILDING THE ROYAL COURT

In 1995, the Royal Court was awarded a National Lottery grant through the Arts Council of England, to pay for three quarters of a £26m project to completely rebuild its 100-year old home. The rules of the award required the Royal Court to raise £7.6m in partnership funding. The building has been completed thanks to the generous support of those listed below.

We are particularly grateful for the contributions of over 5,700 audience members.

English Stage Company Registered Charity number 231242.

## THE AMERICAN FRIENDS OF THE ROYAL COURT THEATRE

AFRCT support the mission of the Royal Court and are primarily focused on raising funds to enable the theatre to produce new work by emerging American writers. Since this not-for-profit organisation was founded in 1997, AFRCT has contributed to nine productions. They have also supported the participation of young artists in the Royal Court's acclaimed International Residency.

If you would like to support the ongoing work of the Royal Court, please contact the Development Department on 020 7565 5050.

THE ARTS COUNCIL OF ENGLAND

## PROGRAMME SUPPORTERS

The Royal Court (English Stage Company Ltd) receives its principal funding from London Arts. It is also supported financially by a wide range of private companies and public bodies and earns the remainder of its income from the box office and its own trading activities.

The Royal Borough of Kensington & Chelsea gives an annual grant to the Royal Court Young Writers' Programme and the Affiliation of London Government provides project funding for a number of play development initiatives.

The Jerwood Charitable Foundation continues to support new plays by new playwrights through the Jerwood New Playwrights series. Since 1993 the A.S.K. Theater Projects of Los Angeles has funded a Playwrights' Programme at the theatre. Bloomberg Mondays, the Royal Court's reduced price ticket scheme, is supported by Bloomberg. Over the past seven years the BBC has supported the Gerald Chapman Fund for directors.

# FOR THE ROYAL COURT

## ARTISTIC

Artistic Director **Ian Rickson**
Associate Director International **Elyse Dodgson**
Associate Director Casting **Lisa Makin**
Associate Directors\* **Stephen Daldry, James Macdonald, Katie Mitchell, Max Stafford-Clark, Richard Wilson**
Literary Manager **Graham Whybrow**
Resident Dramatist **Michael Wynne**
Trainee Associate Directors **Femi Elufowoju, Jnr., Josie Rourke§**
Voice Associate **Patsy Rodenburg\***
Casting Assistant **Amy Ball**
International Administrator **Ushi Bagga**
International Associate **Ramin Gray**

## YOUNG WRITERS' PROGRAMME

Associate Director **Ola Animashawun**
Administrator **Nina Lyndon**
Outreach Worker **Lucy Dunkerley**
Education Officer **Emily McLaughlin**
Writers Tutor **Simon Stephens\***

## PRODUCTION

Production Manager **Paul Handley**
Deputy Production Manager **Sue Bird**
Production Assistant **Hannah Bentley**
Facilities Manager **Fran McElroy**
Facilities Deputy **Adair Ballantine**
Head of Lighting **Johanna Town**
Lighting Deputy **Trevor Wallace**
Assistant Electricians **Gavin Owen, Andrew Taylor**
Lighting Board Operator **Sam Shortt**
Head of Stage **Martin Riley**
Stage Deputy **Steven Stickler**
Stage Chargehand **Daniel Lockett**
Head of Sound **Ian Dickinson**
Sound Deputy **Emma Laxton**
Head of Wardrobe **Iona Kenrick**
Wardrobe Deputy **Jackie Orton**

## MANAGEMENT

Executive Director **Barbara Matthews**
Executive Assistant **Nia Janis**
General Manager **Diane Borger**
Finance Director **Sarah Preece**
Finance Officer **Rachel Harrison**
Finance Assistant **Martin Wheeler**
Accountant **Simone De Bruyker\***
Administrative Assistant **Natalie Abrahami**

## MARKETING & PRESS

Head of Marketing **Penny Mills**
Head of Press **Ewan Thomson**
Marketing and Press Officer **Charlotte Franklin**
Marketing Assistant **Alix Hearn**
Box Office Manager **Neil Grutchfield**
Deputy Box Office Manager **Valli Dakshinamurthi**
Duty Box Office Manager **Glen Bowman**
Box Office Sales Operators **Carol Pritchard, Steven Kuleshnyk**
Press and Marketing Intern **Day Macaskill**

## DEVELOPMENT

Head of Development **Helen Salmon**
Development Associate **Susan Davenport\***
Sponsorship Manager **Rebecca Preston\***
Development Officer **Alex Lawson**
Development Assistant **Chris James**
Development Intern **Marzia dal Fabbro**

## FRONT OF HOUSE

Theatre Manager **Elizabeth Brown**
Deputy Theatre Manager **Daniel McHale**
Duty House Managers\* **Paul McLaughlin, Alan Gilmour**
Bookshop Manager **Simon David**
Assistant Bookshop Manager **Edin Suljic\***
Bookshop Assistants\* **Michael Chance, Jennie Fellows**
Stage Door/Reception **Simon David, Kat Smiley, Tyrone Lucas, Jon Hunter**

Thanks to all of our box office assistants and ushers

\* part-time
§ The Trainee Associate Director Bursaries are supported by the Quercus Trust

## ENGLISH STAGE COMPANY

President
**Jocelyn Herbert**

Vice President
**Joan Plowright CBE**

Honorary Council
**Sir Richard Eyre**
**Alan Grieve**
**Sir John Mortimer CBE QC**

Council
**Liz Calder** Chairwoman
**Anthony Burton** Vice-Chairman
**Judy Daish**
**Graham Devlin**
**Joyce Hytner**
**Tamara Ingram**
**Phyllida Lloyd**
**James Midgley**
**Edward Miliband**
**Sophie Okonedo**
**Katharine Viner**
**Nicholas Wright**

# TERRORISM

by the Presnyakov Brothers

*translated by Sasha Dugdale*

## Characters

*Scene One*
PASSENGER
MAN IN A MILITARY UNIFORM
FIRST PASSENGER
SECOND PASSENGER

*Scene Two*
WOMAN
MAN

*Scene Three*
MAN
WOMAN
SECOND WOMAN
THIRD WOMAN
FOURTH WOMAN
MALE STAFF MEMBER
ELDERLY MAN

*Scene Four*
FIRST WOMAN
SECOND WOMAN
CHILD (*unseen*)
MAN

*Scene Five*
FIRST MAN
SECOND MAN
THIRD MAN
FOURTH MAN
FIFTH MAN

*Scene Six*
FIRST PASSENGER
PASSENGER
SECOND PASSENGER
AIR HOSTESS

## SCENE ONE

*The tarmacked area in front of an airport: instead of the cars usually parked in this area, there are numerous passengers sitting on their bags and cases. Judging by their miserable, huddled poses and their faces, which have stiffened in an expression of resigned desperation and silent hysterics, they've been here quite a while. It seems likely that these wretched people set off for the airport in order to fly somewhere they needed to go: some of them on business trips; some of them on holiday; and some of them, well, just because the time had come for them to fly somewhere. However, something has put paid to their plans and forced all these would-be flyers to stop right here on this inauspicious stretch of tarmac – suddenly a focus of misfortune.*

*On the far side of the tarmac, directly in front of the glass-fronted airport building, stretches a line of armed men. It appears that it is because of this long and rather unsightly line of soldiers that no one can fly. The cordon is an indication of the serious-ness of what is happening. No one is talking – neither the soldiers, nor the passengers. It's very quiet all around. There isn't even the usual roar of planes landing and taking off. There is a depressing feeling of paralysis, acting upon all sounds and signs of life, and it is strengthened by the hardly discernible, yet insistent rustling of the main entrance doors, opening and shutting. A guard in the cordon is standing next to these automatic doors. He was positioned here and he is not able to move from his post, so the doors, which react with great sensitivity to the presence of a human body within their range, are twitching back and forth. The doors will only stop twitching if the soldier moves from his post . . .*

*A new* PASSENGER *appears on the tarmac. Without paying attention to anyone, he walks with a carefully measured pace directly towards the guard, who is standing motionless by the door. Actually it only seems that the* PASSENGER, *who is*

*oblivious of everything, is walking towards the* MAN IN A
MILITARY UNIFORM. *In fact he is walking towards the
doors, which the soldier's bio force has jammed. The*
PASSENGER *appears to know this route well. He walks
almost intuitively, without looking at anything around him, in
his own little world, and this is why he doesn't notice anything
strange about the scene . . .*

MAN IN A MILITARY UNIFORM. The airport is closed.

PASSENGER. Pardon?

MAN IN A MILITARY UNIFORM. The airport is closed.

PASSENGER. But I have a flight to catch – it leaves in twenty
minutes.

MAN IN A MILITARY UNIFORM. Papers.

PASSENGER. Here you are – this is my ticket and . . . erm . . .
here's my passport . . . (*He fusses getting them out and
hands them to the soldier. The soldier studies them and
hands them back.*)

MAN IN A MILITARY UNIFORM. The airport is closed.

PASSENGER. So how am I going to catch my plane?

*The* MAN IN THE MILITARY UNIFORM *remains silent,
and sternly and fixedly gazes straight through the*
PASSENGER.

PASSENGER. Listen, I'm sure you're fed up of explaining
why no one is allowed into the airport, but I happen not to
know. I bought this ticket a week ago and no one warned
me that everything could be just cancelled, because the
airport had closed without warning. So excuse me, but can
you make the effort to answer my questions – they're
completely legitimate.

MAN IN A MILITARY UNIFORM. There is a bomb alert in
the airport and all flights are delayed for the foreseeable
future. When the airport has been cleared of explosive
devices you will be able to enter.

PASSENGER. I will . . . but there won't be much point by then . . . Christ only knows what's going on . . . bomb alerts at the airport. And when will you . . . .What's the point . . .

*The* PASSENGER *mumbles something else whilst moving away from the soldier and sits down on his suitcase next to some other waiting* PASSENGERS.

PASSENGER (*addressing the man sitting next to him, who is perched regally on a checked case*). Do you know what's going on?

FIRST PASSENGER (*looking up at the sky and wrinkling up his eyes*). Of course . . . there's a bomb alert in the airport . . .

PASSENGER. Why . . . I mean, someone must have been arriving or about to leave, someone very . . . Someone they'd want to attack . . . a politician or a scientist?

FIRST PASSENGER (*addressing* SECOND PASSENGER, *who is sitting on the tarmac as he has no baggage. Indeed the only way you'd know he was a passenger is because he is waiting for the airport to open, like the rest*). Are you a politician?

SECOND PASSENGER. No.

FIRST PASSENGER. A scientist?

SECOND PASSENGER. No.

FIRST PASSENGER. Strange. You're the only person here who looks anything like a politician or a scientist . . .

SECOND PASSENGER. Why?

FIRST PASSENGER. Because you haven't got any luggage.

SECOND PASSENGER. So what?

FIRST PASSENGER. No luggage means nothing bothers you. Either it's being delivered, or you don't need it at all, because you're so caught up in your politics or your science you don't think about anything else . . .

SECOND PASSENGER. Well actually I'm not thinking about anything else. But I'm not a politician, or a scientist.

FIRST PASSENGER. Are you worth attacking?

SECOND PASSENGER. No idea . . .

FIRST PASSENGER. I mean, could they have planted bombs in the airport because of you?

SECOND PASSENGER (*nervily*). What makes you think there are bombs planted in the airport?

FIRST PASSENGER (*with irony*). I'm guessing.

PASSENGER. In fact it's what that soldier said . . .

FIRST *and* SECOND PASSENGERS (*together*). The soldier said that?

PASSENGER. Yes, he just told me.

SECOND PASSENGER. I never heard anything like that from them . . . I just know someone left some bags on the runway, and at the moment the bomb disposal people are trying to find out what's inside. And while they're doing that, all the flights are cancelled and the airport is closed.

PASSENGER. All because of some stupid bags?!

SECOND PASSENGER. All because of some 'stupid bags'?! There could be anything in those bags! We could all go up in smoke. And it's naïve to suppose that bombs are planted in airports because of politicians and scientists. They're planted there for everyone, everyone sitting here . . . Because when totally normal, innocent people are killed it's even more shocking than when some famous person is. If the most ordinary people are killed . . . I mean, often and in large numbers, and not at war, but right in their homes and in aeroplanes and on their way to work . . . well then, everything in the country changes, and politicians with their pointless politics and scientists with all their science can go to hell . . .

PASSENGER. To hell?

SECOND PASSENGER. Yes – because no one and nothing can control a world in which ordinary people are killed that often . . . and in such large numbers . . .

FIRST PASSENGER. Yeah – that's right. Why go chasing after the ones with the bodyguards? Because it's so simple to kill an idea, assassinate the sense in things . . . no one guards them, do they? The meaning of life, the big idea . . . it's in people, it's in all of us, and no one's guarding us! Even now they're guarding the airport and not us.

SECOND PASSENGER. The innocent always suffer . . .

FIRST PASSENGER. That's right. The innocent always suffer . . .

*After saying this phrase,* FIRST *and* SECOND PASSENGERS *shake their heads theatrically.*

SECOND PASSENGER. Although one way or another everyone's guilty of something.

FIRST PASSENGER. Still, that's no reason to start bombing everyone.

PASSENGER. Hang on, so where did you get the idea that something in those bags could blow up?

FIRST PASSENGER. They're finding out right now. We're not claiming anything – we're just discussing it. And they (*He points at the soldiers, standing in a line.*) . . . they're finding out . . .

SECOND PASSENGER. But in any case, it's already blown up.

FIRST PASSENGER. Yes, that's right. It's blown up.

PASSENGER. What? (*Looks around theatrically.*) So where's the smoke? The splinters? Ruins? Where are they?

FIRST PASSENGER. It's all inside.

PASSENGER. Inside?

FIRST PASSENGER. Yes. Inside all these people sitting here right now – and the ones who are stopping us going in (*He points at the soldiers.*) . . . Those people standing in the cordon . . . they were torn away from something, from their own lives, whoever they were . . . made to worry, panic, even if they are pretending that they're not scared. But they're cold inside, a nasty little cold draught is blowing through them. They pretend it isn't, but it is, I can see . . . In all of us here something has been broken, we've been made to think about something completely different. And what can we do about it? Eh?

SECOND PASSENGER. And think about the ones out there on the runway at the moment – they're risking their lives opening those bags. There are three suitcases and in every single one of them there could be an explosive.

FIRST PASSENGER. In every one of them?

SECOND PASSENGER. It's not ruled out. There'd be such a blast that even here we'd be covered in splinters.

PASSENGER. You've clearly been here quite a while, you must be absolutely furious. You've obviously got to the point when you know what each other's going to say, because you really seem to have your stories straight.

SECOND PASSENGER (*as if frightened*). Straight?

FIRST PASSENGER (*mockingly*). Straight!

*After this everyone is silent for a while.*

PASSENGER. What's the time?

FIRST PASSENGER. What difference does it make? No one's going anywhere anyway. Where were you trying to get to?

PASSENGER. Does it matter? I just needed to get there. I wanted to fly from this place to another . . . meetings . . . I was given a lift here. My wife packed my bag and saw me off and she'll be waiting for me tomorrow, and they'll be waiting for me there in three hours' time. But it seems I'm not going to be there in three hours . . .

FIRST PASSENGER. You won't!

SECOND PASSENGER. No, you won't!

PASSENGER. So I'm going to be late everywhere, it appears. What shall I do?

FIRST PASSENGER. What indeed?

SECOND PASSENGER. If everything blows up we won't be flying anywhere for a while, till they mend everything . . .

FIRST PASSENGER. We won't be flying anywhere at all, if that happens!

SECOND PASSENGER. If they get rid of the bombs we won't be going anywhere for a while anyway.

FIRST PASSENGER. Really?

SECOND PASSENGER. It'll be two or three hours while they redo the timetable, after all, everything's been put back.

PASSENGER. As long as nothing blows up. I've got to get there, whatever it takes. I've got to get there . . .

FIRST PASSENGER. You'll get there. In about six hours at the earliest, if they defuse the bombs right now.

PASSENGER. Good God. It's madness – what sort of an age do we live in? You don't feel safe anywhere now, only at home . . .

FIRST PASSENGER. At home?

PASSENGER. Only at home now.

FIRST PASSENGER. You hold on to your convictions.

PASSENGER. What do you mean?

FIRST PASSENGER. Who knows what all this will come to? For example, have you any idea what's become of competition?

PASSENGER. Competition? You mean, market forces?

FIRST PASSENGER. Whatever! When someone wants to prove to someone else that he's better than he really is – it's a harmless enough idea, isn't it, and what's become of it?

PASSENGER. What? What has become of it?

SECOND PASSENGER. Competition is all about choice now. If there's something else on offer, why not go for it? It means choosing, it means, horror of horrors, refusing.

FIRST PASSENGER. In theory, yeah, that's right – there is an issue of choice. But, like, they say Pepsi and Coca-Cola are owned by the same company and all this competition stuff is just a clever trick. If you don't buy one, you definitely buy the other, and the owner gets the profit from the lot, because it's all his. All of it!

SECOND PASSENGER. Yes . . . yes . . . yes . . . Hmmm. So in fact this issue of choice is probably just a decoy. It's a sham. Everything has already been decided. Even now.

PASSENGER. Now?

FIRST PASSENGER. Of course. See, I'm boiling with rage inside. I can barely hold back from attacking someone because I'm late, I'm not going to make it on time, and actually I could have died – it's a good thing they discovered those bags on the runway in time. And, in fact, I've got no choice. I've got to sit here and wait until all this madness is over. I'm forced to take part in it all.

PASSENGER. Well I have got a choice.

SECOND PASSENGER. Really?

PASSENGER. Yes. I'm going home. And when everything's returned to normal I'll come back and get my flight. But right now I'm going home because I have no desire to wait here. This doesn't concern me and actually I don't care what happens. I'll wait it out at home, they'll change my ticket, the airline will pay me compensation for the delay and I'll make it to where I wanted to go anyway. I'll be late, but I'll make it. And it doesn't matter whether I'm on time or not as I have a good excuse. They can turn on their TVs and they'll find out that I've got a decent excuse. I'll wait it out at home.

SECOND PASSENGER. You're just trying to convince yourself!

FIRST PASSENGER. Do you think it will help?

PASSENGER (*muttering*). There's a bomb alert in the airport, I'm off home. I'll be back in an hour maximum. Right, that's it. I'm off.

FIRST PASSENGER. So are you really going home?

PASSENGER. Yes. There's no point in hanging around here, this pantomime will go on for ages.

SECOND PASSENGER. For ages.

PASSENGER. Goodbye.

FIRST PASSENGER. But you're coming back?

PASSENGER. Of course I am. I'll get my flight today whatever.

FIRST PASSENGER. Well then, see you soon.

PASSENGER. See you soon?

FIRST PASSENGER. As soon as this madness is over, there'll be another, probably something along the lines of stuffing everyone into one plane, which will race around at the speed of sound dropping us all off where we need to be . . .

PASSENGER. I don't get your stupid jokes . . . what d'you mean by that? What's the point of joking right now?

SECOND PASSENGER. So are they waiting for you?

PASSENGER. Who?

SECOND PASSENGER. Where you're going. There. If there's no one waiting for you why don't you stay?

PASSENGER. It'll be a surprise. (*He collects up his belongings.*)

SECOND PASSENGER. See you then.

*The* PASSENGER *leaves and* FIRST *and* SECOND PASSENGERS *remain seated, waiting.*

## SCENE TWO

*The bedroom in a standard flat. In the middle of the room is a large bed. Slightly to the side is a cupboard with a mirror, and by the bed are bedside tables with lamps and a telephone on one. There's a* MAN *and* WOMAN *in the bed.*

WOMAN. I feel bad . . . (*She's on the verge of crying.*)

MAN. Oh don't start. Anything but that. What's wrong with you, eh? What's this all about – all this emotional stuff suddenly? Some memory upsetting you? Why are you crying for no reason?

WOMAN. I don't know. I feel bad, confused . . . like a used ashtray.

MAN. A used ashtray . . .

WOMAN. I don't know . . . It's like when you've held back for a long time, you really think it's going to be special with that particular man, or with any man in fact . . . you hang on, you fantasise, and then, when it all happens, the second after, this emptiness suddenly descends on you, and now, this is like the whole lot together . . .

MAN. There must be something wrong with you . . . you can't go round being like that!

WOMAN. I don't know . . . But the hardest thing is getting over these first few seconds and minutes. After that, when you start to want it again, it gets easier . . . (*Suddenly shouts.*) And then it all happens again! The whole lot again . . .

MAN. You're a psychopath! How on earth does your husband put up with you?

WOMAN. Habit.

MAN. Habit . . . he puts up with you out of habit . . . And are these hysterics of yours also habit, or did you arrange this show especially for me?

WOMAN. For you . . . for you. It'll pass in a minute. How was it for you?

MAN. Yeah, alright. Could do it again.

WOMAN. Oh God, find another word, anything else . . . are you trying to kill me?

MAN (*theatrically, and with a slightly mournful intonation, reads a poem aloud*).

> Late autumn,
> The rooks have flown,
> The trees are naked,
> The fields are bare,
> Only a strip left to be mown,
> Casts us suddenly into despair,
> As if ears of corn were whispering together:
> We're miserable here in the raging weather . . .

WOMAN. Stop it!

MAN. I dunno. It's helped me ever since school. I say it in my head or out aloud and the time flies past and I think about those ears of corn and not about whatever it is that's troubling me . . . just the ears of corn. It gets better as it goes on, because those ears of corn are sort of waiting for a peasant who hasn't ploughed the land or harvested them, yeah, so they're waiting and calling him and then there's an answer, right, this voice from above or something, says to them, I mean, to these ears of corn:

> He doesn't reap or sow the field,
> Because he is so very sick.
> The hands that tended strips of land
> Have dried to old stick,
> And hang like whips.

WOMAN (*turns right over to face the* MAN *and suddenly climbs on top of him. The violent and yet coquettish way she does this suggests a sudden mood change*). Fancy tying me up?

MAN. Tie you up? What with? I don't wear a belt . . . with his belt?

WOMAN. He doesn't wear one . . . Oh, tie me up with a pair of tights.

MAN. Tights?

WOMAN. Yeah – take some out of the cupboard and I'll lie here like I'm unconscious. (*She rolls away from the* MAN *and pushes him out of the bed with her feet. The* MAN *falls on the floor.*) So I'm lying here unconscious and you tie me up, whilst I'm still unconscious, and I'll come round straight away, but it will be too late and you will possess me completely and I will submit, helplessly.

MAN (*crawls over to the cupboard*). Won't the tights tear?

WOMAN. No, they won't. (*She adopts the pose of a woman who is unconscious for some unclear reason of her own.*) Come on then, they're over there in the cupboard in the middle drawer.

*The naked* MAN *stands up in front of the cupboard and opens the door. In front of him there are a large number of drawers of underwear. The* MAN *opens one, then another, quickly scans the drawer and, discovering nothing made of nylon, he sits down on the ground, deciding to make a more detailed search from the bottom of the cupboard.*

MAN (*pulling a pair of socks out of the cupboard*). Your husband wears long socks. (*He reads the word embroidered on the socks.*) Carpenter . . . They're long ones . . . shall I tie you up with these, then?

WOMAN. They could be dirty. He always chucks them back in with everything else without sorting them.

MAN. With everything else . . . (*He lifts the socks to his nose and sniffs.*) . . . they're dirty . . . (*He lifts them again.*) . . . what a strange smell . . .

WOMAN. Oh, I can't bear it . . . Get on with it, won't you! (*She lies back as if unconscious.*)

MAN. You live in a pigsty . . .

WOMAN (*comes to, irritated*). You keep an eye on your own wife. This pigsty is fine by me.

MAN (*takes a pair of women's knickers out of the drawer and lifts them to his nose*). That's strange – your underwear smells like your husband's socks.

WOMAN (*explodes*). Did he chuck them in with my underwear?

MAN. No, they're in a different drawer, but they smell the same.

WOMAN. Give them here!

*The* MAN *throws the long 'Carpenter' socks and the knickers over to the* WOMAN *in the bed. The* WOMAN *sniffs the knickers first and then her husband's socks.*

That's odd . . . Are you sure they weren't in the same drawer?

MAN. Sure. This is all your stuff – (*He points at one of the middle drawers.*) – and this is his – (*He points at another drawer higher up.*) – and these socks were down here actually. (*He points at the lowest drawer.*)

WOMAN. I don't know. It's probably the cupboard making them smell.

MAN. The cupboard?

WOMAN. Yeah, the smell of wood . . .

MAN. Wood . . .

WOMAN (*throws the socks and the knickers at the* MAN). Put them back and stop sniffing everything, will you? Get on with the business, for God's sake!

MAN (*crosses to another compartment of the cupboard and opens it; in front of him is a space filled to bursting with clothes; the clothes are heaped up in a pile right to the very top of the cupboard*). Your cupboard is full!

WOMAN. And?

MAN (*pulls a crumpled and creased pair of tights from the heap of clothes, then another pair and carries on until he has about five or six pairs*). That's not good!

WOMAN. Why?

MAN. If your husband comes home I'll have nowhere to hide.

WOMAN. He's not coming home.

MAN. Not at all?

WOMAN. He gets back tomorrow.

MAN. All the same, we should have arranged this for when
he was definitely on the plane. Or after he'd arrived in
wherever he was going to. He could have rung to let you
know he'd got there or something. I shouldn't have come
until then. Because this way was ridiculous – me sitting
on the bench, waiting for him to come out of the building
and walk off into the distance. (*He goes over to the bed
and gets up on it, continuing to speak, and starts tying the*
WOMAN's *hands.*) I had fantasies, too – about breaking in
here and making love to you . . . See, I don't care about the
stuff people normally care about. You know, usually, when
it's someone else's wife, you ask, 'Did you give him a
goodbye kiss? Did he hug you?' I don't care about all that
stuff because every one of us does exactly what they want.
And I feel down and empty straight after I come as well,
and then I want to do it again and then I want to eat . . .
It's horribly ordinary, somehow, even the fact that you're
someone else's wife and I'm tying you up . . . should I tie
your legs?

WOMAN (*momentarily coming round and immediately
afterwards 'losing' consciousness again*). Yes.

MAN (*continuing to speak and to tie her up*). I don't want to
think about all this . . . I want to imagine that . . . yes . . .
something untasted and deliciously interesting is lying in
front of me, all tied up, and I'm about to violate it and
nothing will happen to me as a result, because, in theory,
everything has been mutually agreed, although this stuff
wasn't in the small print (*After tying the* WOMAN's *legs
he lays on top of her. He doesn't move for a while and then
he begins the sexual act.*) and I know that I'd be far happier
if I really had the urge to tie someone up and get pleasure
from it, or to secretly sniff someone's underwear or socks

and to get off on it so totally that I could come with the
single thought that I was about to sniff something intimate,
something not mine. That would make me feel good . . . but
I don't like that stuff, I can't get into it, and anyway I've
realised that every little bit of my body is separate from the
other bits and lives its own life, not understood by the rest
of my body. All of it is separate and sometimes, right, one
part of me terrorises another part, yeah . . . at the moment
my mind is making fun of everything that should turn me on.
So I'm rubbing myself on you, but not getting any excite-
ment because it's like I'm in a diving suit, and the fact that
I'm hard and I'll probably come in a minute – all that's my
memory keeping me going, but every time my mind commits
a terrorist act I get closer to forgetting everything and the
first thing that will happen then is that I'll become impotent
and then it'll go further and further and if I suddenly don't
like the smell of someone's underwear or something, then
that'll be it . . . that's it . . . that's it. (*He comes.*)

WOMAN. I've gone numb all over.

MAN. Because of the tights? Shall I untie you?

WOMAN. Because of your words . . . I don't know . . . they're
like chains . . .

MAN. Right.

WOMAN. Turns out you're worse than me. I just felt bad and
I wanted to spoil your mood too, infect you with it – but
you're a nightmare, you're completely hopeless . . . untie me.

MAN. I wouldn't mind a bite to eat.

WOMAN. Great. Untie me.

MAN. I wouldn't mind a bite . . . so I must have something to
eat, that's for certain. After the second go I don't feel so bad
myself because I get up an appetite and suddenly I think
'that was worth doing, after all' . . . it was worth it if only to
get up an appetite . . . I must feed it though, because while
it's still there, there's still hope.

WOMAN. Christ! The more time I spend with you, listening to
all your words, the more I like my husband . . . soon it'll get
to the point where I fall in love with him again.

MAN. I'm saving your marriage.

WOMAN. Untie me.

MAN. Is there anything to eat?

WOMAN. In the kitchen . . . in the fridge. There's a glass bowl covered with a plate. Salad in it.

MAN. Bread?

WOMAN. White? Black?

MAN. Black?

WOMAN. There's no black.

MAN. White?

WOMAN. Baguette.

MAN. Baguette?

WOMAN. It's stale . . . We don't eat bread . . . From the day before yesterday . . . We had guests the day before yesterday. Untie me.

MAN. No I won't untie you. Can I eat in bed?

WOMAN. No. You should eat at the table, but if you don't untie me you can eat in bed, 'cause no one's going to stop you eating in bed.

MAN (*stands up and goes out to the kitchen. He shouts from the kitchen*). I'll eat straight out of the bowl, alright?

WOMAN. Aren't you going to untie me?

MAN. No. This way is more interesting . . .

*He appears in the bedroom with the bowl, chewing. He starts to say something else but he is interrupted by the sound of the phone ringing. The phone rings twice. The bound WOMAN twitches. The MAN stands and looks at the phone. The answerphone clicks on.*

ANSWERPHONE. Hallo. There is no one at home. Please leave a message after the tone. (*The tone sounds and then the machine suddenly fails – it repeats the recorded*

*message and after it the tone sounds and cuts off once
again. A long hissing sound remains . . . )*

WOMAN. There you go – and the answerphone's gone wrong!
Turn it off, will you? That sound drives me mad. (*The* MAN
*stands there, the answerphone hisses – suddenly it quietens
of its own accord and seems to fade out.*) Thanks.

MAN. You're welcome. Only I didn't even touch it.

WOMAN. Never mind. The main thing is it shut up. What
were you saying?

MAN. Who do you think it was?

WOMAN. Who cares who it was. What, were you saying,
would be more interesting?

MAN. Real violence. I was saying that real violence would be
more interesting. I'm not going to untie you. It couldn't
have been him?

WOMAN. Him, her . . . whatever. I'm out!

MAN (*settles on the bed and eats*). I'm definitely out!

WOMAN. That's for sure! What are you going to do when
you've finished eating?

MAN. Have a sleep.

WOMAN. What about me?

MAN. You can do what you like . . . but I'm not going to untie
you yet. I'll have a sleep, rest a bit and then make love to
you again.

WOMAN. You've got it all worked out perfectly . . . almost
too perfectly!

MAN. You don't like it?

WOMAN. No!

MAN. Excellent! Now it's for real . . . none of this playing
around. Is it turning you on?

WOMAN. Not just yet!

MAN. Wait then. (*He finishes eating and puts the empty bowl on the ground, lies down on the pillow and wraps himself up in the blanket.*)

WOMAN. What are you doing?

MAN (*as if he was half-asleep*). Perhaps in a minute . . . or maybe in an hour . . . I'll jump on top of you . . .

WOMAN. What? Are you really going to have a sleep?

MAN. I'll try . . .

WOMAN (*hysterically*). Untie me! Untie me!

MAN. Do you want me to gag you?

WOMAN (*scared*). No.

MAN. Stop shouting then . . .

WOMAN. OK.

MAN. See, you're liking it already.

WOMAN (*hissing like a snake*). Don't sleep for long – I'll get pins and needles in my hands.

MAN. Gag . . . gag . . . horrible word, that – gag.

WOMAN. You understood me . . . pins and needles in my hands.

MAN (*turns onto his side*). Your bed squeaks like a swing –

WOMAN. A swing?

MAN. Yeah, a swing. You've got a swing in your yard and whilst I was waiting for your husband to disappear a kid was swinging for ages, and the swing made this eek-eek noise and your bed sounds just like that . . . It squeaked the whole time when I, when we –

WOMAN. Hey – well I can only check whether it squeaks or not with you –

MAN. Just don't complain!

WOMAN. I'm not!

MAN. You're the victim, I'm the rapist . . . It would be absurd if you started complaining to me.

WOMAN. You started complaining to me first! That's even more absurd – the rapist complaining to the victim that her bed squeaks.

*The* MAN *jumps up from the bed and runs over to the cupboard. He grabs some piece of underwear from a drawer and returns to the bed. He screws up the underwear and stuffs it into the* WOMAN*'s mouth. The* WOMAN *twitches, tries to bellow something out, but the* MAN *stops up her mouth even more firmly.*

MAN. You're really spoiling it for me . . . you're stopping me getting in the proper mood . . . (*The* WOMAN *soundlessly writhes.*) I'll wake up just as you're getting tired and we'll have a good time. You'll have a doubly good time, I'll screw you and untie you. Heaven. (*He covers himself in the blanket from his head down. The* WOMAN *twitches some time more and then calms down. Suddenly the* MAN *throws off the blanket and gets up.*) Can you hear? (*He remembers that the* WOMAN *can't answer.*) Oh . . . Something's hissing. Is it the answerphone or something . . . I didn't turn it off, did I? They're probably still working out a message to leave us . . . Oh well, let them think . . . (*He covers himself in the blanket from his head down.*)

## SCENE THREE

*A small office, a few desks, and chairs in the same colour.*
*The appropriate number of office staff are seated neatly in the*
*chairs. Only one space is empty. A tidy-looking MAN carrying*
*a small file walks over to this very space. The MAN is evidently*
*more senior as his office is in a separate room nearby. Finally*
*looking up from his file, he is surprised not to find the profile of*
*a colleague in front of him, ready to hear out his routine*
*request.*

MAN (*addressing the WOMAN at the next desk*). Er . . . er . . .
  where is she?

WOMAN (*without turning away from the computer*). With the
  psychologist.

MAN. Aah . . . (*He places the file on the desk of the absent*
  *colleague.*) When she gets back . . . I need it calculated by
  the end of the day . . . Will you pass that on to her?

WOMAN. Of course . . .

MAN. Right . . . (*He has a thought and takes another quick*
  *look into the file, closes it and turns towards the WOMAN*
  *he has just spoken to. Again he thinks of something and*
  *picks up some clean pieces of paper from the desk and*
  *covers the file with them.*) Right . . .

WOMAN. Of course . . .

MAN. Right . . . (*He leaves.*)

  *Some times passes. The same tidy-looking MAN comes*
  *back to the desk, which is as empty as before.*

  Not here yet?

WOMAN. No . . .

MAN. Right. (*He leaves.*)

  *After a short time he returns.*

WOMAN. Not here yet.

MAN. I know . . . I just wanted to say that the psychologist isn't in today. It's not his day. He comes in on Wednesdays and Fridays.

WOMAN. Well, I don't know . . . Haven't you been to see him? When he's not there they just play nice music and there's a screen, you can just sit there and she's just sitting there, unwinding psychologically . . .

MAN. If you wouldn't mind just going to get her . . . I mean, how long can you unwind for . . .

WOMAN (*standing up, ready to follow his order*). I don't know . . . they made that room specially so people could unwind, everyone knows themselves when they need to . . . and if it's going to get us into trouble . . .

MAN. Please . . .

WOMAN (*on her way out*). Even the Director said that if you feel the need . . . no one should ignore it . . .

MAN. There's a time and a place . . . you should at least give over a little bit of time to work when you're at work . . . if they didn't teach you that . . .

*The* WOMAN *has already disappeared behind the door and the* MAN *stops talking, realising that no one is listening to him any more. Another* WOMAN *from the office goes over to the annoyed* MAN.

SECOND WOMAN. Sign this . . . (*She stretches out a piece of paper to the* MAN.)

MAN. What is it?

SECOND WOMAN. An estimate.

MAN. I can see that! I'm asking what it's for? Meat? Sugar!?

SECOND WOMAN. What do you mean? (*She begins to shake with irritation.*) We're not a . . . what on earth do you mean by meat?! This is hardly a supermarket.

MAN. Exactly! This isn't a supermarket! So why am I reduced to guessing from the look in your stupid eyes what these papers are you're shoving at me?

SECOND WOMAN. They aren't my papers. Actually I work –

MAN. Alright. (*He takes the estimate out of the* WOMAN'*s hands, scans it quickly and hands it back.*) Come and see me later. I can't just sign it like that . . .

SECOND WOMAN. The thing is, I need it urgently. I've got to put together a bill on the basis of –

*The argument between the tidy-looking* MAN *and the* SECOND WOMAN *is cut off by a scream from somewhere behind the door. Work in the office comes to an abrupt stop and everyone sitting at their desks lifts their heads, waiting to find out whether they've correctly guessed the cause of the sound. The* WOMAN *whom the tidy-looking* MAN *sent out in search of her colleague not long before, runs in.*

WOMAN (*looking around at everyone as if she doesn't understand where she is*). . . .

MAN. What's wrong . . . was that you screaming? Was it?

WOMAN. I . . .

MAN. What's happened? Did you find her?

WOMAN. She's . . .

MAN. She's what? Did you find her or not, I asked?

WOMAN. She's hanged herself . . .

MAN. What?

WOMAN. . . .

MAN. I don't understand. What did you say?

WOMAN. She's hanged herself.

MAN. What do you mean, hanged herself? What do you mean? Where?

WOMAN. There . . . in the relaxation room . . . she's hanging there.

MAN. Wait a minute . . . what do you mean . . . .

SECOND WOMAN. God . . . (*She starts shaking even more.*)

WOMAN. She's hanging there . . .

*Everyone in the office seems to deflate and shrink.*

MAN (*looking around at all the staff as if mentally counting them to work out who's missing*). Right . . . sit here all of you . . . don't go . . . I'll go myself and . . . (*He runs out.*)

*The other staff members all run over to the* WOMAN.

SECOND WOMAN. What? Why . . . why would she do that to herself?

THIRD WOMAN. Have a sip of vodka . . . you just calm down and get a grip on yourself . . .

FOURTH WOMAN. Oh God . . . what about that? Was she on her own there, then? All on her own, was she?

WOMAN. Oh God, I'm all shaken up, I am . . . I mean . . . I only just managed to make myself go and check . . . she was already dead . . . seemed like a while ago . . . seems like as soon as she went out . . . 'cause she went out a while ago. I didn't tell him, did I, that she went out a while ago, because he was just trying to pick a fight, I thought she was just having a rest, or whatever . . . seeing as . . . after all . . . oh God, I've got so much work . . . Right, I've got to fill in that . . . where's my form? Has anyone seen my form? (*She yells.*) Where's my form?

*At this point the* MAN *comes in.*

MAN. Calm her down! I said, calm her down!

*One of the staff members thronging around the* WOMAN *slaps her across the cheek. She quietens but the* MAN *won't stop shouting.*

Calm her down! I said, calm her down!

*The same person who slapped the* WOMAN *slaps the* MAN's *face timidly, but with some force.*

SECOND WOMAN. What are we going to do now?

MAN (*sits down behind the desk and accepts a glass of vodka from a thoughtful staff member*). We need to ring . . . call the . . . to investigate . . . Right away!

*Someone leaves the group, goes over to the telephone and begins to dial.*

WOMAN. We should probably take her down.

SECOND WOMAN. Yeah, only . . .

THIRD WOMAN. What?

SECOND WOMAN. They say it's a bad omen . . .

THIRD WOMAN. Aaah.

FOURTH WOMAN. What is?

SECOND WOMAN. If her head rests on someone then that person will . . . you know . . .

FOURTH WOMAN. No. What?

SECOND WOMAN. What? Neck in the noose themselves, that's what!

FOURTH WOMAN. I didn't know . . . Is that what they say?

SECOND WOMAN. Ha! You must be doing alright if you don't know bad omens like that.

FOURTH WOMAN. I'm doing the same as everyone else. I'm not complaining. But it's the first time I've heard that one.

SECOND WOMAN. Like I said . . . doing alright.

THIRD WOMAN. Maybe then, if someone held her head . . . ?

FOURTH WOMAN. Oh my God oh my God . . .

MAN. Calm down all of you. We mustn't touch anyone . . . We've got to wait. We mustn't touch anything. They'll be here in a minute. They'll do it all . . . Did you call?

THE ONE WHO RANG. Yes! They're on their way!

MAN. Right . . .

WOMAN. We should tell the Director.

MAN. How? He's away.

FOURTH WOMAN. Perhaps he'll have to come back. We should call him back.

MAN (*looking at his watch*). He's already on the plane. Call him back? He's got meetings, contracts . . . Who else can do it, do you reckon? Call him back! Do you know what you're saying? He's got enough problems of his own.

THIRD WOMAN. But this is his problem. Whatever happens, they'll have to have an enquiry.

SECOND WOMAN. They'll have one of those anyway.

MAN. What a nightmare! What a disaster! Go and do a thing like that at work. We've got a reputation to uphold! Goodness – what was she thinking of?

FOURTH WOMAN. You go on thinking about our reputation when a person has died. (*She cries.*)

MAN. Calm down. You've all got to calm down. Now . . . let's think . . . They really will be here soon and we've got to decide what we're going to tell them.

SECOND WOMAN. What for?

MAN. What do you mean – what for? Do you want to spend half your life denying rumours and accusations? People don't just hang themselves.

WOMAN. That's a point. Why did she hang herself?

SECOND WOMAN. Her husband was cheating on her . . .

FOURTH WOMAN. Really?

THIRD WOMAN. Everyone knew perfectly well that her husband was cheating on her. So what? You don't go and hang yourself because of that.

FOURTH WOMAN. Actually I didn't know.

THIRD WOMAN. Well she probably didn't share it with you . . . but I know that she took it in her stride. Straightforwardly and in her stride. We discussed it a lot.

MAN. Really?

SECOND WOMAN. Yes, well . . . It wasn't a secret. At least it wasn't between us.

FOURTH WOMAN. Just to talk about it like that. Well . . .

MAN. Hang on, well that explains it . . . We should . . . we should have a look on her desk to see if she's left a note . . . usually in cases like this they do . . .

*Everyone rushes across to the hanged woman's desk and rummages through the papers.*

THIRD WOMAN. No, there's nothing . . .

MAN (*flicking through a notepad*). In her filofax . . . What's this rubbish . . .

WOMAN. What, what is it?

MAN. It's empty, completely empty. Just the one sentence in the middle . . .

WOMAN. What does it say?

MAN (*reads*). 'Toenails grow faster than fingernails.' . . . Right . . .

*There is a pause. Everyone thinks their own thoughts. The silence is broken by a* MALE STAFF MEMBER *who has been absent all this while. He has been to get some mineral water and he is amazed by what he sees on his return to the workplace.*

MALE STAFF MEMBER (*puts the bottle of water on the desk, smiling*). You're all looking glum. Has someone killed themselves?

*All those gathered there are roused from their own thoughts and turn on the unsuspecting* MALE STAFF MEMBER. *After a pause they start shouting at him all at once.*

WOMAN. Have you completely lost it? Nothing up here, eh? Use your brains just a little bit! I mean, think (*Taps her head.*) just for a second! That's always been a problem for you, hasn't it? You don't listen to anyone. You just don't care about anyone or anything!

SECOND WOMAN. Hanged herself . . . she's hanged herself. Yes, she's hanged herself that's right! And then you get

here! And then you come in! Only first you should stick
your head around the door – (*She taps her head.*) – make
sure everything's alright, before you come in here with your
jokes . . .

THIRD WOMAN. You've got no timing, no timing at all!
Maybe this all seems funny to you, but we only just
managed to bring her around with a drink – (*Points to the*
WOMAN.) – after she saw it all! Not to mention what'll
happen now!

FOURTH WOMAN. We're all sick and tired of your jokes!
What do you mean by it?! You watch some TV . . . (*She*
*points at a place where, it seems to her, a TV might have*
*stood.*) Watch some TV and learn how to joke, and the main
thing, *when* to joke, get yourself some timing! Well, we've
got a right comedian!

MAN (*he interrupts the hissing women when they are about to*
*start gesticulating, so they whisper the ends of their phrases*
*almost silently*). Where have you been?

MALE STAFF MEMBER. I . . . went to get some mineral
water . . .

MAN. And why were you getting it during work time?

MALE STAFF MEMBER. . . . .

MAN. Anyway, we've installed a filter. Don't you like our
water or something?

MALE STAFF MEMBER. No . . .

MAN. What?

MALE STAFF MEMBER. I drink Evian.

MAN. Evian?

MALE STAFF MEMBER. Yes . . .

MAN. So why did we install this filter? Doesn't it work or
something?

MALE STAFF MEMBER. It works, but I like Evian.

MAN. How's Evian better . . . and anyway, how can you tell the difference between mineral waters? Can you tell them by their taste or something?

MALE STAFF MEMBER. Yes . . .

MAN. I see . . . So how is your Evian different from this water that we all drink here?

MALE STAFF MEMBER. . . . .

MAN. So tell me then . . . I mean, if I've got some whim I try to keep it to myself, completely to myself . . . I don't go out during work time, or try to sort out my personal problems when I should be doing something else . . . so why then, do your whims take you over to such an extent that you allow yourself to go out whenever you feel like it, God knows where . . .

MALE STAFF MEMBER (*his lower lip is trembling*). I . . . just . . . went round the corner . . . not God knows where . . .

MAN. What?

MALE STAFF MEMBER. Just round the corner, there's a shop . . . I went . . . (*His face puckers and he starts crying quietly.*) . . . I went in there.

*The faces of the others start to pucker, some more, some less, their eyes start to shine and tears begin to trickle down their faces.*

MAN. Now come on, you explain to me . . . I mean I just don't get it . . . for me personally the simple word 'mineral' on the label is quite enough. For me, that's enough, that's fine, I immediately know that the water inside is pure and good for you, and the name of the water doesn't add anything for me, let alone taste.

MALE STAFF MEMBER (*through his tears*). Don't shout at me.

MAN. What?

MALE STAFF MEMBER. Don't shout at me! If I'm not in the right, I'll make up for it, but there's no need to shout at me.

MAN. What are you going on about, eh? Who's shouting at
you? And don't take that tone with me . . .

SECOND WOMAN (*through her tears*). He shouts at us every
day! Hardly surprising that someone's hanged themselves
here!

MAN. What? What are you saying?

FOURTH WOMAN. That's it! You should keep an eye on
yourself, letting yourself talk to people like that.

MAN. So how do I talk to people, then? How?

FOURTH WOMAN. So that you lose the will to live
afterwards, never mind work.

MAN. What's wrong with you lot, eh? How do I talk to you,
then? Haven't I earned the right to make comments?
(*Addresses the* THIRD WOMAN.) Why is it you don't ever
go out to fetch mineral water or whatever . . .

THIRD WOMAN. It's got nothing to do with mineral water.
We're talking about something completely different. You
don't know how to handle people. How you got that job I'll
never know! I'm amazed!

MAN. Oh right, so it's like that, is it? You're amazed. Well I'm
amazed, too . . . (*He runs over to the* THIRD WOMAN*'s
desk.*) I mean, how old do you think you are?

THIRD WOMAN. What's that supposed to mean?

MAN. I mean, how can a grown-up woman have all this tat
on her desk! The whole desk is covered with it. (*He grabs
some of the little cards, which the* THIRD WOMAN *has
arranged on her desk and shakes them, holding them above
his head.*)

THIRD WOMAN. That's not tat!

MAN. Yeah? So what is it then?

THIRD WOMAN. It's craftwork!

MAN. There we are! Even better! When do people get into all
this stuff, then? It's kids do this stuff usually, if you didn't
know.

THIRD WOMAN. Put them back, please, in their places.

MAN. Don't you worry. I'll put them back, but before you start telling me what's what, you need to work out what's going on with you.

THIRD WOMAN. There's nothing wrong with me.

MAN. Yeah? So what's all this then?

THIRD WOMAN. So who gave you the right to start going through my stuff?

MAN. I wasn't going through it! That's exactly the point! Everyone can see it. If you'd hidden it, then that would be different – but like this . . . you're forcing everyone to stare at them, we all have to put up with looking at your odd little trinkets!

THIRD WOMAN. Who – me? You're putting up with me. Well that's just great.

MAN. Like, why have you . . . (*He turns towards the* FOURTH WOMAN *and reaches out for the photograph on her desk.*)

FOURTH WOMAN. Here you are . . . (*She passes him a photograph in a frame.*)

MAN. So why has this person got an ordinary photo of her . . . (*He looks at it.*) Husband, no funny –

FOURTH WOMAN. It's my brother.

MAN. What?

FOURTH WOMAN. I'm not married. That's my brother.

SECOND WOMAN. But I was told you were married . . . (*She turns to the* THIRD WOMAN.) It was you who told me that!

THIRD WOMAN. That's because she told me herself about her husband, about their honeymoon on the Islands . . .

FOURTH WOMAN (*grabbing the photo out of the* MAN'S *hands*). What islands are you talking about! I'm not married!

THIRD WOMAN. But you told me yourself?

FOURTH WOMAN. What else is there to talk to you about? What else? All you go on about every day are your stupid families and where you go after work with your husbands! (*She puts on a voice and imitates the others.*) 'Nothing to do in town, the same stuff everywhere! I never ordered a private dancer, but they still come over to our table and get undressed and my husband and I were really put out . . . my husband and I didn't like it, my husband and I went on holiday . . . my husband and I . . . my husband and I . . . At the weekend he's taking me . . . at the weekend he's getting me . . . ' Horrible! Horrible . . . the same horrible stuff every day! (*She wipes her face with a paper napkin.*)

WOMAN. Are you jealous or something?

FOURTH WOMAN. Yeah right!

WOMAN. You're jealous of us! How awful! Jealous of what, for goodness sake! (*She picks up the picture from the desk and looks at it.*) Of course it's her brother! The spitting image! How could we have thought . . .

FOURTH WOMAN. Put it back!

WOMAN. Calm down!

FOURTH WOMAN. I said put it back!

WOMAN. I won't do anything. Relax.

FOURTH WOMAN. Don't you understand or something? (*She runs over to the* WOMAN *and grabs the photograph out of her hands.*)

WOMAN. Take it, then. Relax!

FOURTH WOMAN. Cow! (*She puts the photo in her bag.*)

WOMAN. Bitch!

*The door opens and an* ELDERLY MAN *in a red velvet suit enters. The* ELDERLY MAN *is holding in his arms a lapdog of some particularly nasty type whose popping-out eyes appear to be several times larger than the dog itself.*

ELDERLY MAN. Excuse me . . .

*Everyone is silent.*

Excuse me . . . we left our leash behind . . . We left our leash
behind in our office . . . we were on a walk and realised that
we didn't have our leash . . . It's probably in my office, in
the relaxation room . . . it's locked . . . and we need to get
our leash . . . and by the way, why is the office locked,
when I asked that, even when I'm not here, every member
of staff could go and rest, relax . . .

MAN. You can't go in there at the moment . . .

ELDERLY MAN. Why not? Our leash is in there . . .

MAN. One of the staff has hanged herself in there, so you
can't go in there right now.

ELDERLY MAN. I see. Right. Well. I'd better . . .

MAN. Wait a minute . . . hang on, somebody should be here in
a minute. You can wait if you need it . . . They'll take her
down and give you back your leash . . .

ELDERLY MAN. Hmm. (*He waves dismissively and turns to
go, then stops and turns back.*) Maybe you need my help?

MAN. I don't think so really. But thank you . . .

ELDERLY MAN. I don't mind – it wouldn't be difficult for
me . . .

MAN. I don't know. Maybe someone else? (*He turns towards
the staff. Everyone is silent and tries to look away.*)

WOMAN. Thanks. There's no need.

ELDERLY MAN. Oh. Alright then, alright. Goodbye. (*He
leaves.*)

MAN. Goodbye.

EVERYONE. Goodbye.

SECOND WOMAN. How many times has he been asked not
to bring the dog into work!

WOMAN. He says that it helps him; calms down the patients . . .

SECOND WOMAN. Calms them down? That ugly pug! Well, they've hired themselves a right clown. Goes around, getting up everyone's nose – and this is what it's all come to! Has he ever helped anyone, then? I mean, really helped with something?

THIRD WOMAN. Personally I can always take myself in hand . . . Without all this stuff . . . I mean, it's a mystery to me . . .

FOURTH WOMAN. You can, but maybe someone else can't.

THIRD WOMAN. Because you've just got to do things at the right time.

FOURTH WOMAN. What precisely?

THIRD WOMAN. What indeed! You understand me perfectly well.

FOURTH WOMAN. No, I don't understand you at all. You say it straight out, if you mean something in particular.

THIRD WOMAN. Come off it . . . you all understand perfectly well, there's no need for me to explain to any of you here that there's a right time to get married if you want to be able to have normal relationships with people later.

FOURTH WOMAN. Oh! It's like that, is it? So you've been discussing me for a while!

MAN. Listen. I'm lost for words – you've got it all, everything's wonderful, fantastic, but for some reason you all just lose it sometimes . . . I mean, I don't mean . . . what I meant was you all know each other perfectly, you know everything about each other, but you just aren't able to say when something annoys you or gets in your way . . . you store it all up inside, store it all up and then you turn into bombs which blow up at the most awkward moment. Like me, surely I don't shout at you all, like you suddenly announced to me today? Eh? Surely I didn't deserve that? I mean, is it really so hard to bear when someone makes a justified criticism of you?

MALE STAFF MEMBER. And what if it's unjustified?

MAN. Well . . . I suppose, all the same, you could just put up with it . . .

MALE STAFF MEMBER. Hmm . . .

MAN. Well at the end of the day you could just say so, but not in such an overbearing way. Simply because the negative stuff, as I see it, gets stored up all inside and has to come out somehow . . .

WOMAN. We just need to relax more, talk, share our problems . . .

SECOND WOMAN. It would be good if there was someone who could help us unwind.

THIRD WOMAN. . . . Helped us and listened . . . Could even be someone from outside, who wouldn't pass it on to anyone.

FOURTH WOMAN. Just not that clown . . .

EVERYONE. Noooo . . .

WOMAN. With his dog . . .

FOURTH WOMAN. I went in there once and sat down on the couch, thought I'd have a rest . . . but he sits down beside me and gets me to draw a person . . .

WOMAN. A person?

FOURTH WOMAN. Yeah . . . he says, 'Draw me a person, please. I have to test you.' So I scribbled something and the stuff he came out with, I mean, according to him I'm near enough a maniac of some sort . . . Wanker! (*The others nod and giggle approvingly.*)

THIRD WOMAN (*picks up the pictures from her desk*). This is my son's craftwork . . . he loves cutting out, gluing . . . I don't put pictures on my desk for a reason – my husband and my son like him, they aren't photogenic – they come out badly in photographs, or maybe it's that they're not being photographed properly . . . but these pictures are sweet, when I look at them it makes me relax, I get a nice, calm feeling . . . He's a little devil, he drives his Nan mad

the whole time, won't listen to anyone, teases his Dad . . .
He's only quiet when he's doing the gluing . . .

*She looks at the pictures and cries. Everyone goes back to
their desks and starts working again.*

## SCENE FOUR

*A yard with a bench. Two old* WOMEN *are sitting on the
bench. From far off comes the sound of a swing. It is as if
somewhere in the depths of the yard an invisible person is
swinging on a rusty swing – a rusty robot. The robot likes
swinging – so it's not very likely that he's going to stop for a
break at any point and even less likely that he's going to leave
the swing in peace – he's going to be swinging forever. The*
WOMEN *sitting on the bench have probably realized this and
they are trying to get used to the iron sounds piercing their
hearts, and imitate them with the sounds and the droning of
their own voices.*

FIRST WOMAN. Are you dressed up warmly?

SECOND WOMAN. Yes. (*She pulls up her skirt and displays
to the other* WOMAN *her pink woollen longjohns.*) That
Lisa's had a chill in her bladder and she always wears a pair
like this, right over her tights. As soon as there's a breeze,
even a light one, she gets a chill in her bladder straight
away. And then she wees blood. Says it's like someone was
sticking a fork or a penknife into her weehole. There she is
squatting over the toilet and waiting for it to cut its way
through. Five minutes, ten, twenty . . . and then it's got
blood in it. She was wretched with it until she started
wearing these.

FIRST WOMAN. Better safe than sorry.

SECOND WOMAN. Better safe than sorry.

FIRST WOMAN (*turning towards the sounds of the swing,
shouts*). You not tired yet?

CHILD'S VOICE. No!

FIRST WOMAN. Well go on, then, go on. Have a swing.

SECOND WOMAN. Let him swing.

FIRST WOMAN. His parents come home, lock him up in their four rooms and he goes over to the window and looks out, looks at that swing . . . like a dog who hasn't been taken for a walk he looks out. I say to them, let the kid go outside, and they act like they can't hear me, I mean, like I'm there but I'm not. I'm like the noise of the running water when you wash up . . . they notice me when they want something . . . You're a witness.

SECOND WOMAN. Yes.

FIRST WOMAN. Like, I wouldn't wish evil on anyone . . .

SECOND WOMAN. No . . .

FIRST WOMAN. But them . . . You'll see! It's right to my face. Like only yesterday I says to them, if I'm getting in your way . . . if you don't want anyone in the way, well then put me in a home for old people. What do I care? I've seen everything I need to, they're the ones who've got to live and bring up the kid.

SECOND WOMAN. Oh come off it! Honestly, what sort of home would that be, then?

FIRST WOMAN. The usual sort. At least I'll know there that I'm definitely no use to anyone. I mean, look how they treat me here. My own flesh and blood and they talk to me like that!

SECOND WOMAN. What about your daughter?

FIRST WOMAN. What about her? Sleeps with him at night and then repeats his words all day. She does everything he puts into her head at night . . . Sometimes I wonder if it's my own daughter or not.

SECOND WOMAN. Only got yourself to blame.

FIRST WOMAN. Only got myself . . .

SECOND WOMAN. I warned you, when he'd only just started seeing your girl . . . I told you straight off – he'll make trouble for you! He'll get his hands on the lot! You weren't quick enough, you didn't see him coming! And now you'll suffer for it!

FIRST WOMAN (*whimpering*). Yes.

SECOND WOMAN. What in God's name were you thinking of? You know what nationality he is. It's in their blood – commanding, taking control . . . and you allowed the blood to mix . . .

FIRST WOMAN. Lovely child, though.

SECOND WOMAN. Lovely! But so what? Grow up just like his Dad! Degenerate!

FIRST WOMAN. Stop it!

SECOND WOMAN. Come on. If you don't manage to drag him out from his Father's influence he'll grow up just the same.

FIRST WOMAN. But he's got a good job, money coming in!

SECOND WOMAN. How much of this money do you see? Any? There you go. Where does he dance – in a casino?

FIRST WOMAN. A club, in the restaurant . . .

SECOND WOMAN. So he'll keep the job as long as this fashion for ethnic holds. They get a load of these ones, like your son-in-law and ask them to dance and sing, all in their . . . national style. And no one understands a word of it, do they, what they're singing and dancing, 'cause everyone's on drugs, the in-crowd and they're in seventh heaven – someone in front of them wriggling and howling something they don't understand. The ones who've got money – they get high on it, on all this ethnic, and invest in the ones like your son-in-law. These ethnics then reckon that someone has really understood the stuff they're singing, when in fact no one gives a monkeys – it's just they've made it the fashion, 'cause no one cares about normal songs and dances, they've all got brains like Aero bars, full of holes – and to them it's boring. No one gets off on simple understandable human language or straight culture anymore. Druggies, druggies all around, they've got the money, these producers, network marketing managers, supervisors . . . all working for drugs . . . My whole pension goes on paying for my mobile and food, and they're working to pay for the drugs as well. Just wait and see, this fashion for ethnic will pass and your son-in-law will be back sweeping the yard or nicking scrap metal – which is, after all, what these shepherds in their ribboned shirts should be doing.

FIRST WOMAN. So, if they chuck him out of work, I'll have to support them, will I?

SECOND WOMAN. No one'll ask you. You'll be in slavery, sweetheart. Or they'll just drown you in the bath and take the flat for themselves.

FIRST WOMAN. Oh my God, are you serious . . . what am I going to do . . .

SECOND WOMAN. Here you are! (*Takes a little phial out of her coat pocket and stretches it out towards the* FIRST WOMAN.)

FIRST WOMAN. What's this?

SECOND WOMAN. This is war, d'you understand? It's time to move from preventative measures to ground attack! In this war it's the first to make a move comes out the winner. One of these tablets in his soup or his tea every day and in just six months daughter, grandson and his favourite Gran will be one happy family. All that'll remain of the son-in-law are . . . happy memories.

FIRST WOMAN. Look at these round pills. Is this poison or something?

SECOND WOMAN. Lozenges, love. Of course it's poison – don't worry – you won't be found out – it's already tried and tested – personally, by me! And your son-in-law is just a crook, my husband was way worse!

FIRST WOMAN. So you –

SECOND WOMAN. Helped him! Helped him, or he'd have been around another twenty years, preparing to meet his maker.

FIRST WOMAN. He was such a nice man –

SECOND WOMAN. Nice? That nice man ruined my whole life. It's only the last year I've started to live like a real person. Freedom, my own flat, all the kids sorted out and no one bothering me.

FIRST WOMAN. How many tablets? One?

SECOND WOMAN. One.

FIRST WOMAN. What about two? Would it be twice as fast?

SECOND WOMAN. If you try two – I'm telling you now – I won't be bringing you food parcels in prison. He'll have shit running in his veins instead of blood and they'll work out it was you straightaway . . . so you be patient, let it take its time . . . And then no one will guess what happened . . . just one tablet a day! Do you understand?

*A* MAN *carrying some suitcases approaches the bench where the* FIRST *and* SECOND WOMEN *are sitting and sits down a little way from the* WOMEN, *puts the suitcases down near him and looks down at the ground. He tenses his forehead and mutters something. His eyes are already wet and the wetness is just about to trickle down onto his cheeks. The* WOMEN *break off their conversation and look discreetly out of the corners of their eyes at the* MAN *sitting next to them. The* FIRST WOMAN *calls out theatrically in the direction of the squeaking swings, still squinting at their strange companion.*

FIRST WOMAN. Are you tired yet?

CHILD'S VOICE. No!

FIRST WOMAN. Well go on, then, go on. Have a swing.

SECOND WOMAN. Let him swing.

*The* MAN, *unable to restrain himself, starts crying.*

FIRST WOMAN. What's wrong, eh?

SECOND WOMAN. Hey, hey, hey . . . now then . . . come on . . . get a grip!

FIRST WOMAN. Here's a hanky. Wipe your eyes. (*She offers the* MAN *a hanky.*)

MAN. Thank you.

*The* MAN *wipes away his tears. The* WOMEN *stare at him, expecting that he will unburden himself to them any moment now.*

MAN. Yes . . . (*He loses himself in thought and looks into the distance. His tears stop flowing and his eyes dry up.*) So what's up with you?

FIRST WOMAN. With us?

SECOND WOMAN. What do you mean?

MAN. Well, why are you sitting here, what are you waiting for?

FIRST WOMAN. I'm giving my grandson some fresh air!

SECOND WOMAN. And I'm getting a bit of fresh air . . . what's wrong with that? I've got the whole day ahead!

MAN. Well then . . . (*He stands up, picks up the suitcases and walks off.*)

FIRST WOMAN. Well look at him!

SECOND WOMAN. Honestly, do I have to account for what I'm doing out here? It's my husband I account to, and he's hardly going to ask me!

FIRST WOMAN. I always sit here! My grandson is swinging over there, and so what?

SECOND WOMAN. Those bossy types, I've always managed to get away from them, and now, thank you very much, I'm free, I do exactly what I want! So now does every so-and-so think he's got the right to ask me questions and give me instructions? Do I have to write reports or something now?

FIRST WOMAN. I took him into the yard one block along for a walk. The swings are better over there. These two military types came up and asked if some green car was ours.

SECOND WOMAN. Who does he think he is . . . taking his suitcases out for a walk . . .

FIRST WOMAN. I says to them, it's not . . . why you asking?

SECOND WOMAN. He was probably late somewhere and annoyed about that, and we got in his way . . . I'm not leaving this place ever.

FIRST WOMAN. So then they asked for my name and address. The car's tyres had been let down, they said, and no one knows whose it is, so they start asking if I knew anything or saw anyone get in it or let down the tyres.

SECOND WOMAN. I'm not waiting for anything any more. I've done my bit of waiting . . . and then this one turns up here and starts asking . . . I did my bit of waiting thirty years ago and now I've stopped waiting.

FIRST WOMAN. I says to them that I hadn't seen who got into the car or who let down the wotsits, I've got other things to worry about – my grandson is on the swing over there and why should I give my name to any old so-and-so?!

SECOND WOMAN. I don't even report back to my grown-up children where I've sat and where I've been, so why does some other bloke think he's got the right? They've got their lives, I've got mine – it just so happened that their lives started from me, but I don't make any demands on them because of that! And they know they won't get anything from their Mother.

FIRST WOMAN. All the same they took down the lot, wrote it down, even my postcode! See what I mean! So I don't go to that yard anymore – keep well clear! There's a swing here as well. Not a bad swing. Give us those pills, then.

*The squeak of the swing suddenly stops.*

SECOND WOMAN. Take them. (*She passes the* FIRST WOMAN *the bottle of tablets.*) Who is he, anyway? What's his name? With his suitcases! Nowadays they have to check out anyone carrying suitcases.

FIRST WOMAN. What's that on your forehead?

*She stares at the forehead of her elderly friend. She has a bright red dot shining and trembling slightly, right in the middle of her forehead, like the symbol of marriage on an Indian woman. Only this isn't a symbol of marriage, but a laser sight.*

SECOND WOMAN. What?

FIRST WOMAN. Red dot. Come here. (*She spits on her finger and tries to rub the dot off, but the red dot, like a ray of sun, escapes from her finger and settles slightly higher.*) I need a hanky.

SECOND WOMAN. He took it off with him! Well I never! Took us for a right old ride, didn't he. Stop it, will you? (*She pushes away the hand of her friend from her forehead.*)

FIRST WOMAN. Oh – it's disappeared! Oh – it's back again!

SECOND WOMAN. What's that, then?

FIRST WOMAN. Oh – I think it's one of those laser sights . . . Like a sniper's aiming at you . . .

SECOND WOMAN. What for?

FIRST WOMAN. To shoot you.

SECOND WOMAN. Oh my goodness! (*Jumps up and runs around the bench, hides behind the* FIRST WOMAN *and peeps out from behind her back.*) Look, what's that your grandson is pointing at us?

FIRST WOMAN. Oh! That's what his dad gave him – it's only a toy, that laser sight.

SECOND WOMAN. So it's started already! That's how it all starts, with toys! Tell him to put it away! (*Hides behind* FIRST WOMAN.) Tell him!

FIRST WOMAN (*shouts at the* CHILD). What are you up to, eh? (*Turns to her friend.*) Don't be scared, it doesn't shoot, it just aims.

SECOND WOMAN. Oh right, it aims – it just aims and then it shoots! (*She shouts to the disobedient* CHILD.) Put it away, do you hear? Move it away from us!

FIRST WOMAN (*to the* CHILD). Sit down and have a swing! Sit down and have a swing, love!

SECOND WOMAN. He's not listening!

FIRST WOMAN. Right, I'll teach him! (*She rushes over to the swing with a shout.*) Didn't I tell you to put that thing away? Put it away! Sit down and have a swing! Or I'll take you home!

SECOND WOMAN (*getting up*). Look at what blood makes people do. Just in their blood, and that's it, nothing you can do, doesn't matter how you bring them up, you need to poison the lot of them, every single one . . . (*Shouts at the* FIRST WOMAN.) Go on, break it! Break it into bits, so he won't ever play with it again! (*She runs over to the swing.*)

## SCENE FIVE

*In the shower changing rooms at the base of one of the military police divisions. Steam from the showers penetrates into the changing rooms and envelops the countless lockers and low benches. A* MAN *with an athletic build is sitting on one of the benches in front of an open locker. He is squeezing white cream out of a long, large tube onto his palm and then rubbing it carefully on his toes. There is an impatient knocking and rattling from the next locker as if someone was locked in there and trying to break open the door from inside. At this point the door opens with a bang and two more young* MEN *run into the changing rooms with towels around their waists. One is holding a box of washing powder, the other runs over to his locker, digs around in it and gets out a sheet of white paper. Together they go over to the locker, from which the noise is coming, laughing and egging each other on. One shakes out some powder on the paper and the other one lifts it over to the chinks in the door of the locker and blows as hard as he can. There is the sound of coughing from inside the locker. The* MEN *guffaw, pleased with their little joke.*

FIRST MAN. Chemical weapon attack!

SECOND MAN (*shouts into the locker*). Don't breathe!

THIRD MAN (*rubbing cream off his hands*). Why do you keep getting at him?

FIRST MAN. 'Cause he's a fucking meatball!

SECOND MAN. Ravioli man! (*They both roar with laughter and lift the paper with the powder on it up to the locker and blow. Someone starts coughing loudly in the locker.*)

THIRD MAN. Where've you been today?

FIRST MAN. A fire. Someone blew up a block.

THIRD MAN. What was it like? (*The person locked in the locker begins to knock frenziedly, the noise drowns out their voices.*) Come on, open it – you've worn him down between the two of you.

*The* SECOND MAN *opens the locker. A puny naked* MAN *falls out. He looks much older than the* MEN *who locked him up. He gets over his coughing fit and then goes over to his locker, opens it and starts dressing, muttering the whole time . . .*

FOURTH MAN. Bastards . . .

SECOND MAN. You should be thanking us . . . See, you're ready for anything now – even chemical warfare! (*Roars with laughter.*)

THIRD MAN. So what had happened, then?

FIRST MAN. Gas explosion.

THIRD MAN. Accident?

FIRST MAN. No, it's not clear yet, but most likely it wasn't an accident. The whole floor was destroyed and the explosion was in one of the flats – the experts have been digging away

and the first signs are that it was a set up. Someone switched
on the gas, all the taps . . .

*The* SECOND MAN *is now digging away in his bag. He
takes out a photograph and shows it to the* THIRD MAN.

SECOND MAN. Hey, look at what I snapped! Lovely, eh?
Lovely.

THIRD MAN. Whose hands are those?

FIRST MAN. Look, hands and feet are tied to the bed, and in
the middle – nothing! Hey, wow!

THIRD MAN. You're maniacs! You collecting for an
exhibition?

SECOND MAN. Look – the limbs stayed with the bed, 'cause
they were tied to it . . . but the body was blown away . . .
they found it outside, amazing, eh? (*He roars with laughter
and sticks the photo right under the* THIRD MAN*'s nose.
The* THIRD MAN *pushes him away and the* SECOND
MAN *brings the photo up to the eyes of the* FIRST MAN.)

FIRST MAN. Put it away! I can't sleep doing this work as it is.

FOURTH MAN. You're all sick.

SECOND MAN. What's wrong with you, eh? (*He gives the
photo to the* FIRST MAN *and takes his towel from his
waist. He folds it double and twists it up. Then he twirls it
above his head, approaches the* FOURTH MAN *and whips
his thighs with energy.*)

FOURTH MAN (*shouts out hysterically*). Leave off me!

SECOND MAN. I'll leave off you in a minute! I'll leave off
you so bad, you'll do for our photo exhibition. I'll just rip
your legs off and stick them in your locker and we'll take
their picture and call it 'Legs in a Locker' (*Roars with
laughter.*)

FIRST MAN. No – we'll screw them to the bottom of the
locker and then it'll stand on his legs. (*They both roar.*)

FOURTH MAN. What do you want from me? Why do you get
at me the whole time? (*He starts to cry.*)

SECOND MAN. 'Cause you're a meatball!

FIRST MAN. Ravioli man!

SECOND MAN. Seen your ears recently?

FIRST MAN. Was your Dad an elephant, then? Your Mum get too close to the cage at the zoo? Then she had you!

SECOND MAN. Elephant!

THIRD MAN. Alright, that's enough! Let him get dressed and disappear, the moaning he makes, I can't stand it anymore.

*The SECOND MAN whips the FOURTH MAN with the towel again. The FOURTH MAN presses himself against the locker and remains silent.*

SECOND MAN. Come on then! Give us a moan!

*The FOURTH MAN suddenly turns around to the SECOND MAN and with all his strength, jumping slightly, gives him a swinging punch right in the face. The SECOND MAN falls over and lies there for some time working out what has happened. Then he jumps up suddenly and runs over to the FOURTH MAN, lifts his hand and punches. The FOURTH MAN dodges the blow adroitly and gives his aggressor another good punch in the eye. The SECOND MAN shouts out in rage and leaps onto the FOURTH MAN, knocking him to the floor. Their bodies weave into a ball which rolls wildly from one side of the changing room to the other. At this point another fat, elderly MAN comes into the changing room. He is only wearing a t-shirt and trousers. He has bare feet and he is holding his tunic and boots in his hands. The MAN stops in amazement and looks at the fighting MEN, and then at the FIRST and THIRD MAN. They jump up and rush over to the FOURTH and SECOND MEN and attempt to part them. Then all four stand to attention along the bench in front of the FIFTH MAN. The FIFTH MAN goes over to his locker, puts the boots in at the bottom, hangs up the tunic and takes off his trousers. He wraps a towel around his waist. Without looking at the four standing to attention, he issues his command.*

FIFTH MAN. At ease! (*Turns towards them all.*) Not tired yet?
Lots of energy, eh? Eh? Can't find a better use for your
hands, eh? Give them something to play with. That'll relax
them. (*Addresses the* SECOND MAN.) You fight with him
today, and tomorrow he might not drag you out of the rubble
or from the epicentre, eh . . . You go on jobs together . . .
(*Creaking, he sits down on the low bench.*) Or maybe he'll
just give you a little push from behind. (*He winks at*
FOURTH MAN.) Eh? And that'll be it – tragic accident
on the job – and all because of your own stupidity . . . Sit
down. (*They all sit down.*)

*The* FIFTH MAN *remains silent for a long time, then he
asks a question, but it isn't clear to whom it is addressed.*

Did you take any photos?

*They are all silent.*

Come on then, show me, I saw you snapping away. Show
me!

*The* SECOND MAN *gets up and goes over to his locker. He
searches for the photo. The* FIRST MAN *runs over to his
locker and gets out the photo and stretches it out to the*
FIFTH MAN, *who has a good look at it before handing it
to the* SECOND MAN.

A woman.

OTHERS (*together*). A woman?

FIFTH MAN. Nails are painted.

SECOND MAN. Painted? (*Stares at the photo and then passes
it to the* FIRST MAN.)

FIRST MAN. You've got eagle eyes – how on earth can you
tell red nail varnish from blood?

FIFTH MAN. You can tell – when you've seen as much as me,
you'll be able to. (*He addresses the* THIRD MAN.) And
where did they send your lot today?

THIRD MAN. The airport.

FIFTH MAN. What was going on there?

THIRD MAN. The usual, suitcases on the runway . . .

FIFTH MAN. Did they explode?

THIRD MAN. No, they were empty.

FIFTH MAN. Empty?

THIRD MAN. Yeah, someone left empty suitcases.

FIRST MAN. Deliberately?

SECOND MAN. Why would they have deliberately left empty ones?

FIRST MAN. Well, perhaps they were giving a warning? To scare everyone.

THIRD MAN. Well they succeeded. We were stuck there for three hours, probing it all with the robot.

FIFTH MAN. Well, we had . . . did the boys tell you?

THIRD MAN. Yes . . .

FIFTH MAN. Could have been an accident, could have been bloody anything. Someone turned on the gas, two people in the flat, then a spark from the doorbell set it off . . .

THIRD MAN. The doorbell?

FIFTH MAN. Yeah, from the doorbell . . . some kid, little fool . . . old woman and her friend were chasing him to give him what-for for some reason or other . . . anyway, he was going mad, running up the stairs, ringing all the doorbells on his way, so the people would come out of their flats and stop the women, ask why they were ringing and he could keep running and get away.

THIRD MAN. Cunning!

FIFTH MAN. Yeah right, cunning – so he rings the doorbell of this flat and is blown away . . .

FOURTH MAN. Probably scared they wanted to beat him up, probably . . .

FIFTH MAN. Yeah, got their own back, alright. They're still alive, themselves. Not sure about the kid yet.

THIRD MAN. Old cows! What the hell were they playing at?

FIFTH MAN. We questioned the women and asked them why they scared the kid so much that he started racing around the block, and one goes, 'We do that a lot, but nothing's ever blown up before.' I mean honestly . . . and the other one hasn't said a word so far, it's probably the shock . . . She won't say anything, just keeps writing – some man's name and then asks him to forgive her, writing and writing away . . . 'Forgive me', and this bloke's name. Then she looks around and shows us the bit of paper and moans . . .

THIRD MAN. Anything can happen after something like that . . .

FOURTH MAN. That's right, some people turn into beasts after an experience like that . . .

SECOND MAN. What?

FIFTH MAN. So why is it you keep taking photos of all this stuff?

SECOND MAN. Why? I don't know, like, for a laugh, and then maybe we can do an exhibition or something, like, 'This is what not to do', so everyone looks at all these horrible sights and is horrified and is more careful in future . . .

FIFTH MAN. You're talking shit.

SECOND MAN. Yeah? . . .

FIFTH MAN. Yeah! Look how beautiful it is! (*Takes the photo from the* FIRST MAN.) Eh? If it hadn't been beautiful, you wouldn't have taken a picture of it. That's right! If someone looks at these pictures they see beauty in them and not horror. And so off they go to bring this beauty into being. And that's how everyone is infected. Because after all, it's not about how many die in all this – the explosions, murders, terrorism . . . it's about something else, way more frightening – this is the beginning of a chain reaction. Everyone, I mean everyone, is infected. Innocent people get killed – so then the innocent become infected and the peacemakers go about doing violence with the zeal of the converted. And no one wants to stop. No one! But all these little thoughts, they're neither here nor there. It's even funny, how run-of-the-mill they are! Still, your idea is damaging, these photographs . . . an exhibition . . . it's like the empty suitcases on the runway. Eh? Everyone studies them, analyses them – but they don't explode here and now, they explode later, in each person, in their life, each one differently. What? . . . Because it's so easy now – my friend told me this story, about how late at night he threw his old dog off the balcony . . . easier that way, the sweepers will clear it up in the morning, no hassle, just chucked it off, and that's that, an old dog. Horrible, isn't it? I'm telling you that as an example of something terrible . . . because it is terrible . . . So maybe, if you see what I mean, you go off and tell your friends that you've got this colonel whose friend is a sadist, and you tell them what he did with his dog, and they go off and tell their friends and then someone sees the point of it, I mean, after all, it's handy – no paying to have it put down – just out on the balcony and over! And if no one had told him, would he have thought of it by himself, eh? Or he thinks, someone else has done it already, so why shouldn't I go ahead?

FOURTH MAN. So you reckon even talking about it, showing it should be forbidden . . . You reckon, yeah, that once it's happened, that's it. Bombs, murder, violence – let it go on. So long as we're kept in a cage, right, kept so we know nothing, nothing, about it . . .

FIFTH MAN. I reckon that unless you show this lot (*He points at the* FIRST *and* SECOND MAN.) you mean business, they'll fuck you over totally soon. Whenever I see you lot off duty they're always on your back. Eh? What? You sort out your own problems first, and then think about other people's. So stop the arguing. Alright, relax!

*He gets up and goes into the shower room. The* FIRST, SECOND, THIRD *and* FOURTH MEN *start getting dressed. Suddenly the* FIFTH MAN *comes back in, goes over to the others and, completely unexpectedly, starts to sing:*

Happy Birthday to you!
Happy Birthday to you!

Happy Birthday, Mister President!
Happy Birthday to you!

Eh? How did that sound?

SECOND MAN. Like Marilyn Monroe.

FIFTH MAN. Right! No one, no one, sings that from the heart,
with real feeling. At all those anniversaries, concerts, at
home . . . they all try to sing it like she did back then to the
President. Did you know that the President and the rest,
they were all waiting for her that night, but she was late,
and she was . . . she needed a fix, she was desperate . . .
Like, I mean, think about it, she needed help, help first,
work it all out later . . . That voice, those gestures – typical
of heroin addicts . . . there's your happy birthday for you.
And everyone took it as the norm, everyone wanted to copy
her. Imagine . . . Eh? Alright, relax . . .

*He goes out.*

## SCENE SIX

*The half-empty business class cabin in an aeroplane. A
PASSENGER is sitting in one of the seats. There is no one
next to him. The PASSENGER is trying to fasten his seatbelt
without looking. He keeps missing and trying again. He
succeeds the fifth time. The FIRST PASSENGER goes over to
him.*

FIRST PASSENGER. Have you fastened your seatbelt?

PASSENGER. Yes . . .

FIRST PASSENGER (*sits down in the spare seat next to him*).
However much I fly, I can't ever seem to do up the seatbelt
at all, I just can't get it, what goes in where, I twist it round,
this way and that, all until someone helps me.

*The PASSENGER is silent.*

FIRST PASSENGER. Will you help me?

PASSENGER. Of course. (*He leans over and fastens the seatbelt.*)

FIRST PASSENGER. What soft hands . . .

PASSENGER. What?

FIRST PASSENGER. Like a boy's, plump little fingers, not all men's are like that . . .

PASSENGER. Really?

FIRST PASSENGER. Usually it's just the stylish ones, the very stylish men who have hands like that, if you get my meaning.

PASSENGER. No.

FIRST PASSENGER. Oh well. Never mind.

*The* SECOND PASSENGER *appears in the aisle.*

SECOND PASSENGER. Well, fancy meeting you . . .

FIRST PASSENGER. Fancy meeting you . . .

SECOND PASSENGER. Fate, eh?

FIRST PASSENGER. That's it, fate. (*They both laugh.*)

SECOND PASSENGER (*to the* PASSENGER). You've done your seatbelt up.

FIRST PASSENGER. And me! I've done mine, too!

SECOND PASSENGER. By yourself?!

FIRST PASSENGER. No, I was helped.

SECOND PASSENGER. With no consequences? (*They both laugh again, in the way that old friends might laugh at a private joke.*) So, I'm by the window, am I? (*He squeezes past the two seated* PASSENGERS *and sits down by the window.*) Don't have to do up your seatbelt by the window, it won't make any difference anyway, by the window . . . and not just by the . . . . (*He looks out of the window.*) Hey, the right-hand engine isn't working . . .

PASSENGER. What? We should tell someone . . . (*He leans over towards the window and twists his head around to look out.*)

SECOND PASSENGER. Joke! I was joking!

PASSENGER. That's not funny.

SECOND PASSENGER. Not funny?

FIRST PASSENGER (*to the* PASSENGER). Actually he's even more scared than we are, he just isn't showing it. That's why he's making such stupid jokes.

PASSENGER. Very stupid jokes.

SECOND PASSENGER. Look, I'm really, really sorry – He's right: I'm very scared. I mean, take a look – just a thin partition wall and out there – sky. Just the thought of it makes my head spin and I witter away, witter, to distract myself and even to stop myself thinking at all . . . 'Cause if you think about it, it could send you out of your mind. Easily.

PASSENGER. Perhaps you should have a drink?

SECOND PASSENGER. Unfortunately I don't drink.

FIRST PASSENGER. Well, I'll have one.

PASSENGER. Me too.

FIRST PASSENGER. Press it then.

PASSENGER. What?

FIRST PASSENGER. The call button.

PASSENGER. Oh yes. Strange, they're supposed to be walking around, asking if we want anything . . . strange . . .

SECOND PASSENGER. And us all meeting here, that's not strange?

PASSENGER. What?

FIRST PASSENGER. He just means that something not in the least strange seemed strange to you.

SECOND PASSENGER. Whereas you just missed a much stranger thing altogether.

PASSENGER. The way you talk. It's as if you're twins or even as if there's just one of you and not two . . .

FIRST PASSENGER. Really?

SECOND PASSENGER. Really?

FIRST PASSENGER. Where are you flying to?

SECOND PASSENGER. Me?

FIRST PASSENGER. Yes.

PASSENGER. Where's the hostess?

FIRST PASSENGER. So where are you flying to, then?

PASSENGER. Me?

FIRST PASSENGER. Yes. So why is it then? How come we've all been stuck together like this?

SECOND PASSENGER. Hey! Listen! The engine really doesn't work.

*The* FIRST PASSENGER *and the* PASSENGER *both lean across to look out of the window.*

PASSENGER. It's on fire!

FIRST PASSENGER. We've been hit!

PASSENGER. What are you talking about? There's no war on – who could have hit us?

SECOND PASSENGER. My! Who's a bit self confident! How long ago did you come aboard the plane?

PASSENGER (*looking at his watch*). Half an hour ago.

FIRST PASSENGER. Half an hour? Do you know what could have happened in that time?

SECOND PASSENGER. The world could have been turned upside down.

FIRST PASSENGER. And, if that's how things are going, we'll land in a completely different world.

SECOND PASSENGER. If we land at all.

PASSENGER. What are you going on about! Where's the air hostess? Where are we flying to? Where are we going to land? I've got to get out! I've got to go back!

FIRST PASSENGER. Calm down! Calm down!

SECOND PASSENGER. How are you going to get out? That's too easy! Come on, be patient.

PASSENGER. I've got to . . . I . . . I . . .

FIRST PASSENGER. What? Come on, tell us.

PASSENGER. I've got to go back and turn off the gas.

SECOND PASSENGER. The gas?

FIRST PASSENGER. You mean you went home, turned on the gas and then forgot to turn it off again?

PASSENGER. See, I got home and they were lying there, he was asleep and she was tied up, with a gag in her mouth. First of all I thought, who did this to her? And then I realised . . . They were having fun, having fun and suddenly I walk in. She's tied up and he's asleep. She saw me, saw me and understood everything, felt it. I started closing all the windows, quietly, so I didn't wake him, all the windows, and then I turned on the gas, all the taps, out of the oven, and she understood everything, all of it, but she couldn't do anything at all, except moan, she moaned . . .

FIRST PASSENGER. Hmmm.

SECOND PASSENGER. Why are you telling us all of this?

FIRST PASSENGER. Do you think it makes up for it, or something?

SECOND PASSENGER. You got your own public confessional going, eh! If it's all the same to you, we don't feel too good either!

FIRST PASSENGER. Exactly!

SECOND PASSENGER. Why don't we all just start digging up our past misdemeanours . . . who did what to whom . . . Will that make you feel better?

PASSENGER. No. But maybe it'll make you feel better?

FIRST PASSENGER. It's disgusting. It's too late to get it all back now, isn't it? It's disgusting to feel sorry for doing things you can't undo, it's too late to change. What stopped you thinking about all this when we were still on the ground, eh? Because today you could have acted differently – you could have – but you acted as you did, and this now, your present, is what you made it yourself.

SECOND PASSENGER. That's right! When everything's fine and there's no upsets, no one wants to think about anything.

FIRST PASSENGER. You're in a right old mess! You're in a right old mess, do you understand, and you have been for a while, a long while.

PASSENGER. Who made her do it? What was missing from her life? We lived well, we got on together, loved each other, what more did she want?

SECOND PASSENGER. Don't be stupid! That's not what it's about! Take a look at yourself for a start, what's going on in your life. After all, something happens to you every day, doesn't it? You must pass the time somehow, find things to occupy yourself. You've got to start with the small things, the people like you. Because every day each person is moving closer to the fate they deserve . . .

FIRST PASSENGER. If anyone here overheard us, they'd laugh. Even as they burnt with the plane, they'd laugh. What a mess we're in! Deluding ourselves that somebody out there is going to kill us, when actually it turns out we kill ourselves, don't we? Not all at once, of course, but in slow motion, like a film.

PASSENGER. Hey, stop right there! What are you talking about? We've got to save ourselves, put out the fire! Why!? Why is everyone just sitting here!

*He jumps up and rushes around the cabin. The few* PASSENGERS *in business class remain placidly in their seats.*

Why?!

FIRST PASSENGER. Stop running around like a headless chicken for God's sake! You worked all of this out a long time ago! What's the point in putting out the fire, what's the point in saving this plane, when more will burn tomorrow?

SECOND PASSENGER. Go on then, run! Put out the fire! But what's waiting for you when you land? At home, at work . . . what's waiting for you? It's terrible, terrible to feel vulnerable like this, but actually you're the one who's to blame!

PASSENGER. Stop it! That's enough! I don't want to hear any of this! You're insane! Don't keep going on like that! I read all that stuff, I had it at school, heard it from my Mother! When I was little . . . when I was little! . . . (*He falls on the ground and cries. An* AIR HOSTESS *comes up to him.*)

AIR HOSTESS. Please fasten your seatbelt.

PASSENGER. What?

AIR HOSTESS. Please fasten your seatbelt. We are taking off. Would you like anything?

*The* PASSENGER *sits down in his seat. He looks around. There is no one in the cabin apart from him and the* AIR HOSTESS.

PASSENGER. Eh? (*Looks out of the window.*) Aren't we flying yet?

AIR HOSTESS. We're taking off. Would you like anything?

PASSENGER. No . . . thank you . . .

AIR HOSTESS. Are you alright?

PASSENGER. Yes, thank you . . . Thank you.

*The* AIR HOSTESS *leaves him. The* PASSENGER *gets out a mobile phone and dials a number with shaking hands. There is the sound of a tone and then an answerphone clicks on.*

ANSWERPHONE. Hallo. There is no one at home. Please leave a message after the tone. (*The machine fails and there is a hissing.*) Please leave a message after the tone . . .

*There is a long tone and the* PASSENGER *is silent. He is waiting for the tone to end and thinking what he will say, but the tone doesn't end, and the* PASSENGER *can't get his thoughts straight in order to work out what to say after the tone.*

**A Nick Hern Book**

*Terrorism* first published in Great Britain in 2003
as an original paperback by Nick Hern Books Limited,
14 Larden Road, London W3 7ST in association with
the Royal Court Theatre, London

Typeset by Country Setting, Kingsdown, Kent CT14 8ES
Printed and bound in Great Britain by Bookmarque,
Croydon, Surrey

A CIP catalogue record for this book is available from
the British Library

ISBN 185459 731 0